WORK OF THE CHURCH

GETTING THE JOB DONE IN BOARDS AND COMMITTEES

DAVID SAWYER

Judson Press ® Valley Forge

WORK OF THE CHURCH: GETTING THE JOB DONE IN BOARDS AND
COMMITTEES

Library of Congress Cataloging-in-Publication Data

Sawyer, David R.
  Work of the church.

  Bibliography: p.
  Includes index.
  1. Church management.   I. Title.
BV652.S25 1986   254   86-21431
ISBN 0-8170-1116-1

Contents

OTHER BOOKS IN THE SERIES:

Introduction: The Church As an Organization to Do Christ's Work

*". . . the whole frame grows through
the due activity of each part."*
—Ephesians 4:16

The church meeting is over. At least half of the members leave with a feeling of frustration. After a lot of talk and plenty of inspiration, another two hours were spent without accomplishing much. These members want to "get things done" in their church. They just don't know how.

This book offers current knowledge from the field of organizational science presented in a nontechnical, commonsense fashion combined with biblical and theological insights gained from fifteen years of experience as pastor, teacher, and consultant. The assumption behind the book is that lay members along with pastors, educators, and denominational executives can help move their churches from faith to action by applying these organizational principles in the context of biblical and theological understanding.

Three different words have been used to describe the field of study suggested in this book. Some people refer to it as management. Others call it church leadership. I prefer to speak of this area of expertise as church administration. Taken from the Latin *ad* meaning "to" or "toward" and *ministrare* meaning "to serve," the term evokes images of the biblical steward, the servant who runs a household. Administration is defined here as "directed servanthood" and refers to the ministry of organizational direction. In church work the pastor, other staff members, and the church officers take on roles of administration as special functions. Yet they are not the only persons who administer. Any member who attempts to get work done in a church is acting out a service to God, to the people of God in the church, and to the world. Such a person might be called an *ad-minister-ator.*

Often people forget that the church is an organization which requires administration. We readily recognize the church as a community of believers who worship together and who care for and support each other along life's way. We acknowledge the church as a spiritual entity, called into being by God, nurtured and guided by the Holy Spirit. We remember that the church is a spiritual reality which cannot be completely defined in human terms. At the same time, the church is a corporate, human reality with form and structure. Its members and leaders are human. This image of the church as a human organization does not detract from its spirituality. Instead, the church's humanness reminds us of its high calling to be the incarnation of the Spirit in a very real world.

With this rationale, I want to suggest a definition of the term "organization" which will be helpful in understanding how to get work done in a church:

ORGANIZATION is a grouping of persons characterized by

- Systematic interdependence of activities
- Division of labor and of authority
- System of communication
- Goals held in common

Take those points one at a time and they don't seem so difficult to comprehend.

Systematic interdependence of activities. In an organization the activities of one person or group of persons are unavoidably connected to the activities of another group. How the choir performs affects the plans of the pastor and worship committee for the Sunday liturgy. If the evangelism committee recruits new members for the church but other members make those newcomers feel unwelcome, the work of the committee is short-circuited. The Epistle to the Ephesians refers to interdependence in the verses quoted at the beginning of this Introduction.

Division of labor and of authority. Not everyone is an usher or a teacher. Different people assume various tasks in the church. The authority in the church is also clearly defined according to tradition or constitution. Chapters 1 through 5 of this book are based on the division of labor and authority.

System of communication. Chapter 6 describes communication as the process that holds an organization together.

Goals held in common. Every organization has a set of goals, directions, or purposes that guide its activities. When a group no longer agrees on goals, it is in danger of falling apart. Chapter 7 deals with conflict over goals or directions in a church.

Our definition of "organization" applies to any structure from the United States government to a children's baseball team. A church, however, is a distinct type of organization which may be defined more specifically in this way:

CHURCH is a voluntary organization in a particular place, whose goal is the growth or expansion of a central religious value.

Such a definition helps the reader to realize that in this book the term "church" means a particular or local church congregation. Its denominational affiliation is not as important to this discussion as its organizational health. The church is voluntary in the sense that people choose to belong or not, and usually work together without the restraints found in business organizations where people do what the boss says or get fired.

The goal of the church may be stated differently in various places and denominations. A familiar term for a goal is "mission," pointing to the biblical notion that the church is sent (*missus*—sent) to carry the message of faith to all people everywhere. One denominational constitution describes the church as "a fellowship of believers which seeks the enlargement of the circle of faith to include all people and is never content to enjoy the benefits of Christian community for itself alone."[1]

A danger in studying church administration from an organizational perspective is that a heavy emphasis placed on the internal workings of the church may crowd out attention to the purposes for which the church exists. Albert Curry Winn in his study of the Gospel of John affirms the incarnational reality of the church as an organization, but he also raises the question of priorities.

> Where is most of the time of church members spent when they do what they call "church work"? Are they out in the world in the work of proclamation, justice, compassion, and peace? Or are they oiling the ecclesiastical machinery? Examine the church budget. How many dollars go to serve the needs of the world, and how many to maintain the institution of the church? Have we gone out into the world in any meaningful way, or are we still hiding in the sanctuary?[2]

The principles and experiences in this book are presented with the belief that awareness of organization and skills in administering can free the church from some of the pitfalls that hinder fulfillment of the tasks for which it has been sent into the world.

1

Getting Work Done as Followers

"[Jesus] said to them, 'Follow me.'"
                    —Matthew 4:19(RSV)

"Each of us has been given his gift. . .
[for] the building up of the body of Christ."
                    —Ephesians 4:7,12

The pastor crumpled up a couple of small pieces of paper and carefully dropped them on the floor in front of the gathered children. Through two puppets, the pastor discussed the way each person can be a servant to all by doing even the lowest kind of work around the church. "Picking up litter," one of the puppets said, "can be a noble service to God and to others." When the children were dismissed, none of them paused to pick up the paper at their feet.

Here is a parable on why work does not get done in a church. No one is willing to take the little jobs. Many books and articles have been written about leadership in the church, but little has been said about followership. An exception is Robert Greenleaf's *Servant Leadership*. According to this author, if members of a church begin to think of themselves as servants who are willing to do whatever is necessary for the church to function, the church will move ahead to become a force for change in society.[3] What better motivation can there be for doing work in the church than love of God and love for each other? Even church leaders with years of experience would be helped in their activities by remembering that each Christian is first a follower—a follower of Jesus Christ.

Assessing Our Gifts

Serving as a follower is not a simple task. Anyone who has tried to organize people, whether a community group or a church, knows that identifying the unique abilities of the followers is essential to help them serve the organization well. Few of us have any clear idea about how our particular gifts can help an organization. Not long ago, an elderly woman told me about a young woman whom she many years earlier had asked to work in a women's circle in her church. The younger woman protested strongly that there was absolutely nothing she could do that could be worthwhile to the church. Thankfully she was finally persuaded. When I was told the name of that woman, I recognized her as one who over the years has grown into a strong servant of the larger church as parliamentarian and records-keeper for a regional governing body of her denomination. The older woman recognized her gifts and thus helped develop one of the fine servants of the church.

If we picture the follower as an instrument of God, the idea of assessing people's gifts becomes clearer. There are, according to the Bible, a variety of gifts or abilities provided to get work done in the church (Ephesians 4:11-12). To be useful they must be applied to the tasks for which they were intended. Trying to get a pair of scissors to drive a nail, or an ice pick to serve rice from a bowl is wasteful. With self-awareness, however, the follower can identify the interests, abilities, and experiences to help him or her find a place to serve in the church.

In order to help the self-assessment process, a partial listing of gifts is given here as a supplement to the biblical catalogs (Ephesians 4, 1 Corinthians 12).

Encouragement—the ability to offer support and acceptance to others who are doing work in the church; the inclination to praise the contributions of others.

Listening—the gift of hearing what is said and what is felt, of giving others the sense of being heard and understood.

Prayer—the gift of regularly speaking with God on behalf of the church, its members, its work, its prosperity.

Expressing opinions—the gift of stating one's values, beliefs, or positions on matters important to the church.

Being in touch—the gift of rapport or being in touch with other members of the church, serving as a link among members and leaders, able to be the person who calls the pastor about someone who is ill or troubled.

Raising questions—an ability to ask for relevant facts or assumptions behind church discussions.

Responding—the ability and willingness, when requests are made or invitations issued, to offer one's services. "No response" can be devastating to a church program.

Participation—the ability to enter into group or social activities, to "give it a try" even if one has never done something like that before.

"Handi-work" or "people-work"—some have more interest in activities that involve physical labor or paperwork, while others are better at dealing with people.

This list is intended to help you begin the self-assessment process. You are encouraged to be creative in naming your own gift or gifts. If you find this hard to do, try conversing with a pastor, a wise friend, or a supportive group of friends.

The purpose of our gifts is to serve the well-being of the church. Any follower who insists on exercising a gift in a manner that is ultimately damaging to the church or to its unity, purity, or ecumenicity, has forgotten the words of Ephesians 4:12 in which gifts are described for "building up the body of Christ." The following words from a modern declaration of faith summarize this point well:

> The early Christians recognized
>   a diversity of abilities and functions
>   as gifts of the Spirit.
> Some were tempted to use these gifts
>   to serve their own needs and ambitions,
>   to form elite groups who looked down on
>   others.

> But the gifts were given for the common good,
>   to build up the community in love
> and to equip it for its mission in the world.[4]

Getting Along with Church Members

Sometimes work cannot be accomplished in a church because people who need to cooperate on a task are not compatible with each other. Their complaints may be petty or significant. Their reasons may be years old or brand new. It's tough to be a follower when you have to walk side by side with someone who is irritating. Thus have many bowed out of the active followership in the church.

During the Nazi period of the 1930s a young German pastor headed an underground seminary in which ministers for the confessing church could be trained. They lived in an intense Christian community based on their understanding of the Bible. In his book about that experience, *Life Together,* Dietrich Bonhoeffer described the way a "dream-wish" for community often inhibits the development of actual common life. Bonhoeffer went on to write that a pastor or a member of a church "should not complain about his congregation, certainly never to other people, but also not to God. A congregation has not been entrusted to him in order that he should become its accuser before God and men."[5] The congregation was given to us by God, and thankfulness is a more appropriate response than complaint.

A sense of annoyance with a fellow church member can

also be a symptom of false superiority. Is the other member a sinner? Well, so am I. Am I forgiven by the grace of God through Jesus Christ? Well, so is my brother or sister. Indeed, we who feel so much friction among ourselves are all anointed by the same salve of God's love. To use another metaphor, the harmony that I may not be able to accomplish in my own heart can be, and is, accomplished in the heart of God.

In many organizations such as business and government, people work together effectively whether they like each other or not. By some deep mystery, however, those same people may bring the wheels of progress to a complete halt when called upon to work with someone they don't like in the church. Certainly there are people who are difficult, perhaps even impossible to work with, but a genuine follower will find another way to serve instead of dropping out.

John Savage's work with church dropouts indicated that people left church because they were either apathetic (they blamed others for the problems they saw) or bored (they blamed themselves for any problems that arose).[6] While these categories are helpful for reaching out to the already alienated, boredom and apathy can also become excuses for members who simply refuse to get along with other members. The present chapter is written as a guide for followers who are determined to be active in the church and who long to get things done.

A final element in getting work done as a follower is trust. Some church members take their responsibilities so seriously that they attempt to question every decision and every program that is proposed. When a group or committee has studied an issue, carefully considering the various alternatives, and has recommended a course of action, others sometimes treat the proposal as irresponsible. Such suspicions can inhibit healthy motivation for action in a church. They reveal an inner attitude which is unbecoming to a follower. Perhaps persons are taking themselves too seriously–unable to trust in God.

In secular politics we find the old image of the smoke-filled room, where deals are made through compromise. In church politics also, some people are accused of making decisions in a smoke-filled room. Certainly some church decisions may arise from less than noble motivations, but the distrustful member operates on an assumption that "a smoke-filled room is any place where a decision was made and I was not present."

A call for trust of one's cofollowers is not a request to suspend common sense in the course of church activity, however. If a proposal is made which clearly violates a commonly held value or has failed to take an important factor into account, someone needs to speak up. Nevertheless, a good follower assumes that each other follower is as conscientious as possible and has the best interests of the church in mind.

When I developed a questionnaire to test the communicational climate of churches, one of the six essential elements of healthy climate I discovered was "warmth, trust, and consideration."[7] Three questions on the test demonstrate ways this element appears in church life:

- Most members of this church trust one another and offer support to one another.
- Most members of this church get along well with each other and enjoy doing church work.
- Most church members appear to be particularly considerate of their fellow members.

In churches where members answered these questions positively, people were more likely to participate in church meetings. Attendance at meetings was higher, and people felt freer to speak up and make a comment which was helpful to the proceedings. Warmth, trust, and consideration help members be good followers.

A Higher Calling

Several years ago an insurance company promoted one of its services to clergy with a full-page magazine advertisement showing a man at the top of a ladder painting the eaves of a church building. In bold print were the words: "When Pastor Martin answered a higher calling, this is not what he had in mind." The picture and the words grabbed attention because of the instant recognition of their truthfulness. Truly we look to service in the church as a higher calling. Truly, too, many of the necessary activities of church work, for both clergy and laity, are not glamorous. Further, it is true that churches sometimes fail to allocate their human resources well. Is it good stewardship for a person who spent seven years in college and seminary to be spending valuable abilities and time in tasks that others would do with more efficiency and greater enjoyment?

A deeper truth about that advertisement is that there is no higher calling than to be a servant of all. All who would be "ad-ministers" in the church start out as followers of Jesus Christ. Church administration is directed servanthood, and no one is too good to perform the less glamorous tasks.

Based on this understanding of the calling of the follower, this chapter has invited administrators to look inward to identify the gifts they bring to the various services of the church. Followers, in turn, have been encouraged to look outward to recognize possibilities for getting along with and trusting other members of the church.

In an age of impersonality the church offers an opportunity for individuals to make a unique contribution to an important social institution. The church as the body of Christ is a corporate whole which is built from the variety of members who work together to carry out the goal of expanding faith among its own members and in society. Welcome to this ministry!

2

Getting Work Done
as a Leader

"Men judge by appearances
but the LORD judges by the heart."
—*1 Samuel 16:7*

Becoming a leader is an exhilarating, uncomfortable experience. For all the truth of the last chapter about each person having a special work to carry out in the church, eventually someone has to play the role of leader. Whether as leader for a half-hour discussion group in a workshop or as head of the annual bazaar, suddenly the work of other people depends on one person. One cannot be sure whether to thrill at the chance to make a special contribution or shudder at the prospect that it might make a major disaster. As the fellow said after being "run out of town on a rail"—if it weren't for the honor of it, he would have preferred to walk.

The Leader as Servant to the Servants

The leader's job is to help other people get work done in the organization. This servant concept, which can take some of the sting out of the leadership experience, is especially important in a voluntary democracy. Most church members want to be involved and feel important. They also want someone to inform them what their task is and to help them find ways to carry it out. Here is where the term "ad-minister" comes into focus. A leader's role differs from that of other workers by helping them to carry out their tasks.

Nothing is more discouraging than to see the person who chairs the building and grounds committee mowing the lawn regularly or mopping the floors every time they need it. Of course there are exceptions, but such solo activity should not happen regularly. A few leaders want the job done so perfectly that they can trust no one else to do it. Others simply have not learned to ask people to help with the general workload. Both types of leaders are candidates for rapid burnout. More significantly, they deny others an opportunity to serve in meaningful ways.

The primary activity of a leader is "head work": to plan and assign work and devise ways to motivate the workers, and then to show them appreciation and supportiveness as they work. Because these mental tasks are unseen, leaders may feel guilty about not "doing anything." Without the organizing thought, however, little is done satisfactorily.

Among the more difficult mental activities of a leader is that of making judgments about the workers. While most of us avoid such judgments whenever we can, a leader regularly engages in knowing people "by the heart" rather than by appearances.

Assessment of Task Maturity. A common mistake of leaders is to assume that a person assigned to a task wants to do it, knows how to do it, and is able to do it. These three factors gauge the maturity of a worker for the task. Note that the type of maturity meant here is *task maturity*. A person may be quite mature in years, or in the faith, or in an occupation, yet when faced with the task of teaching a class or planning a worship service, such a person may have low maturity.

The first factor is motivation. To what extent does the worker have an interest in carrying out the task reasonably well? A worker who lacks a desire to reach a goal or meet a standard would be judged immature for that task. Perhaps a worker has accepted a task only because of the recognition such a position affords, or even because he or she did not know how to say no. Further motivation may be needed.

Second, the worker is judged on knowledge of the task itself. To what extent does he or she realize the scope or responsibilities? Are all necessary steps to accomplishing the task clearly understood? A Sunday school teacher needs to know the importance of arriving at the classroom ahead of time to arrange materials and greet students, needs to understand how to adapt printed materials to the abilities of students, and needs to be aware of standards the students must meet (recite the Twenty-third Psalm from memory by November 1, for instance). Such know-how maturity is gained through training, experience, or a combination of the two.

A third appraisal of maturity is made on the issue of ability. This, of course, includes skill. One may know how to type, yet be very low in typing skill. Regardless of motivation which prompts the typist to keep pecking away, low speed and high errors will contribute more to frustration than to achievement. Or someone may know how to operate the buttons on a phone system, but inability to communicate pleasantly with callers indicates low task maturity. The worker's personal or environmental limitations are also factors in ability. Occupational schedules, living arrangements, personal obligations and demands on time, and even the ability to organize or prioritize responsibilities seriously affect one's task maturity. Consider the familiar type of man or woman who could handle any of several important church tasks with great skill, but who takes on too many to get them done properly.

The leader does the difficult brain work of determining each worker's task maturity and providing appropriate motivation, explanation, and guidance.

The Adaptable Leader

Does one style of leadership serve better than another? Recently the following comments were heard from three different church members.

"One thing about our pastor is he doesn't run too tight a ship. He gives you a chance to do your job. But after awhile he checks in with you to be sure you're getting it done."

"Seems like the preacher always has to have things done his way."

"You'll notice our minister never tells us what he wants us to do. He leaves it up to us."

All three comments referred to the same pastor. As I checked out those comments, I discovered that the pastor used a different leadership style with different workers. With the first member, he recognized a moderately high task maturity that needed little direction other than an occasional phone call to see how things are moving. On the other hand, having judged that the second worker had inadequate knowledge and ability for a task, the pastor became very directive and authoritarian towards that person. The third worker, however, was highly motivated and thoroughly experienced in the task, and an opposite style of delegation was appropriate. This pastor had achieved a level of effectiveness as a leader by adapting the leadership style according to the task maturity of particular workers.

Task and Relational Behaviors. Only in the past fifty years have teachers of administration recognized the importance of combining two very different ways of behaving as a leader. On one hand a leader may be mainly concerned for the structure of the tasks to be performed, pushing for quality and quantity of work output. On the other hand, a leader may exhibit primary consideration for the relationships people have with each other when they work together. Most leaders have some degree of mixture of these two concerns. In the late 1940s and early 1950s a group of researchers at Ohio State University put these two behaviors together in studies summarized in a graph shown in Figure 1.

Leaders' styles could be charted from low to high levels on the horizontal axis for task behavior and the vertical axis for relational behavior. For example, a leader who tells workers exactly how their jobs are to be done, when to do them, and what standards of quality she expects would be marked at the high end of task behaviors. If that same leader pays practically no attention to the relational needs of workers, such as their need to feel important, their need for recognition of work well done, and their need to have a say in their work, she or he would fall to the low end of relational behaviors. A high-task, low-relational leader style of this type is indicated by its location in quadrant one (Q 1), the hard-nosed sector. Another leader might be contrasted as giving a high degree of attention to the relational needs of workers while paying very little attention to the tasks to be accomplished. That leader's "country club" style would be charted in quadrant three (Q 3).

The Ohio State studies described ways in which leadership styles differ by task and relationship behaviors. They did not give any clues, however, to effective ways of adapting leadership styles.

The Adaptable Leader theory added a third dimension to the graph called worker maturity. As devised by Hersey and Blanchard, the third dimension is charted on a maturity continuum from very low task maturity on the far right to high task maturity on the far left, shown in Figure 2.

Figure 1—The Ohio State Leadership Quadrants[8]

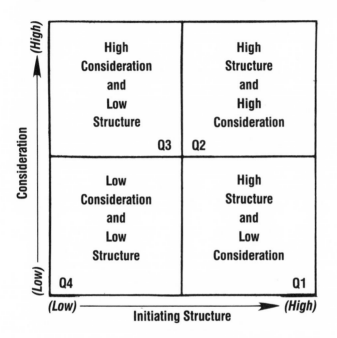

Figure 2—Task Maturity Scale[9]

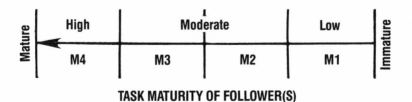

Figure 3—Adaptable Leader Chart[10]

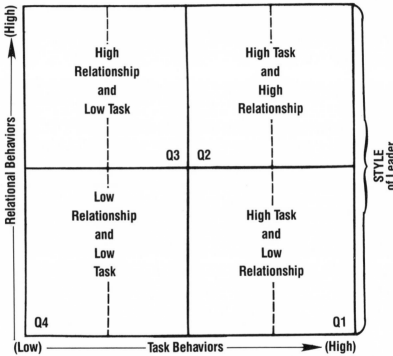

By combining figures one and two, the most effective adaptations of leadership style can be charted with a bell-shaped curve on the four quadrants of Figure 3.

The Adaptable Leader chart and the theory behind it can be tremendously helpful to a leader in a voluntary democracy such as a church. Church members cannot be hired or fired for their skill, experience, or motivation. So the leader follows leadership styles appropriate to the workers' task maturity.

For a worker who has planned adult programs in the past and who is excited about possibilities for a Lenten series of activities (M 4), the leader sits back and lets the worker go his or her own way (Q 4). If the members of the stewardship committee have never carried out a capital funds campaign before, or are not too sure they even want to do it (M 1), the leader's task is to convince them of the necessity for the task (the church needs $25,000 for a new room) and to teach them the steps of good fund raising. The leader will coach the committee and prod them to accomplish each step along the way (Q 1). Next year, if the same committee stays together, their experience and motivation probably will have improved markedly after raising $30,000 (M 2), and the leader will have less pushing to do. Leader style then may require more encouragement and attention to the relationship needs on the committee (Q 2).

When the chair of the fellowship committee returns from an out-of-town trip to discover committee members bickering among themselves to the detriment of their programs, a quick look at the Adaptable Leader chart could give a clue to what is wrong. Suppose the chair has been using a "country club" style of leadership (Q 3) with lots of support and encouragement, but the members appear to be lacking in knowledge about how to carry out their jobs. A few of them even seem to have little understanding of how important the fellowship activities of the church are. The level of task maturity would be at the lower end of the chart (M 2). For the immediate future the leader would be wise to become more directive and at the same time continue the high relationship behaviors. Emphasize what they have done well, and sell them on the importance of the monthly coffee hours. Listen to their complaints with understanding, and very specifically spell out their duties at the family night carry-in dinners. Such high task and high relational behaviors could be called the "selling" style of leadership (Q 2).

The Adaptable Leader theory is not as complex and sophisticated as the graphs and references to university research might suggest. Most behavioral science theory is just common sense that someone wrote about in a book. An easy way to check this out is to reread this section, and then explain the Adaptable Leader theory to a friend. Chances are the friend will say, "Well of course everybody knows you have to change your leadership style to fit the situation." Unfortunately, what everybody knows is not the same as the way everybody acts. Several years ago I became enthusiastic about the "facilitator" style of leadership which was very relationally directed (Q 3). I expected the people with whom I worked to be as competent in church work as they were in their various professions. I made sure everyone felt good about their roles, and encouraged everyone to communicate with each other and with me. Beyond that, I left the work pretty much up to them. When annual evaluation time came around, I was in hot water up to my clerical collar. I discovered I had used the same style of leadership wherever I went and, like a favorite old flannel shirt, it was not appropriate for every occasion. The lesson of the evaluation was that I had not been an effective servant of servants because I had not been adaptable.

The risen Christ said to Simon Peter, "If you love me, feed my sheep." The church continues to need disciples who will serve the sheep by providing leadership adapted to varying conditions. Thus is the work of the Kingdom accomplished.

3

Getting Work Done Through Committees

"The task is too heavy for you; you cannot do it by yourself. You must yourself search for capable, God-fearing [people]. . . and appoint them. . . ."

—*Exodus 18:18,21*

In the previous chapter we saw the building and grounds committee chairperson mowing the church lawn all alone every Saturday. Compare that scene with the image of Moses as his father-in-law found him, struggling with the administration of the Israelites in the wilderness. Whatever else he might have been, old Jethro was wise in administration. His suggestion set in motion a model of church administration that has lasted for three thousand years: the appointment of committees to divide up the work of the congregation.

How many committees does a church need? In smaller churches (two hundred members and fewer), the official board acts as a single committee to oversee the worship, nurture, mission and maintenance of the congregation.

In much larger churches (over 1,000 members) there may be many committees, each with as many as nine or ten members. The ideas in this chapter and the next will require some adaptation to the number and size of committees and boards in a particular church.

Why Work Through Committees?

Committee work has been the object of ridicule in modern times. Yet what traditional value has not faced questioning? Whether they are named committees or departments, bureaus or agencies, or even task forces, the principle is the same. We work through committees to share the work more effectively, to increase congregational participation, and to assure that the work will actually be carried out.

Committees Share the Work and Increase Effectiveness. Unilateral work and decision-making by a single person is not only lonely, but research indicates that it is clearly less effective than a group working together.

In experiments that you could try in your own committee training sessions, researchers gave each member of a committee an assignment to be done alone:[11]

Below is a list of ten occupations which have been ranked by a public survey as to trustworthiness. Your task is to rank these ten in the same order of trustworthiness as the people in the survey. The question in the survey was: "In their dealings with the public, can members of this occupation usually be counted on to tell the truth to the best of their knowledge, regardless of the reason?" Place the number 1 by the occupation you think was ranked as the most trusted, place the number 2 by the second most trusted occupation, and so on through the number 10, which is your estimate of the least trusted of the ten occupations.

_____	U.S. Army generals	_____	auto mechanics
_____	clergy	_____	law enforcement officers
_____	used car sales personnel	_____	politicians
_____	physicians	_____	TV repairers
_____	lawyers	_____	TV news reporters

Next, the whole committee is brought together and told to make a group decision on the ten occupations. The group is told they must reach a substantial agreement on the placement of the items, with three rules: (1) no averaging, (2) no "majority rule" voting, and (3) no "horse trading." When the group has finalized its ranking, the survey answers may be given (based on a 1971 study).

1. Physicians
2. Clergy
3. Lawyers
4. Law enforcement officers
5. TV news reporters
6. U.S. Army generals
7. TV repairers
8. Auto mechanics
9. Politicians
10. Used car sales personnel

In nearly every case the group scores are closer to the survey scores than the individual scores. This exercise shows the advantage of full discussion of a matter by a group or committee.

A few years ago the head of a church board of trustees

wanted to install an energy-saving device on the church's heating system. The idea had not been studied by a committee. The head trustee had facts and figures on how much the device would save and pay for its cost over three years. On the basis of this one person's research, and lacking any other information, the board approved the purchase and it was installed. Later a member who had not been consulted on the decision, reported to the pastor that she could have secured the same device for one-third the cost authorized by the board. That was an expensive lesson in utilizing committees to study any project or proposal carefully as a group, to insure that the most effective decision is made.

An old joke goes that "the camel is a horse built by a committee." The comparison of the sleek beauty and efficient speed of a Kentucky thoroughbred with the lumpy, plodding, cantankerous dromedary is funny. It is true, of course, that getting too many designers into a planning decision can result in a hodgepodge product. But don't be too quick to laugh at the camel committee. If a committee had been given the assignment of designing a beast to carry heavy loads over long distances under dry and sandy conditions, they would be wise to recommend the camel as the best possible solution. For overall effectiveness and sharing the workload, I still recommend Jethro's model.

Committees Increase Participation. In a voluntary democracy, the members want to feel they are represented in important decisions. They like to see their opinions and those of their colleagues taken into consideration before programs are planned or major changes are made. One way would be to poll the entire membership on every decision that comes before the board. For some major decisions for which a simple set of choices can be presented, polling is not a bad idea. Most problems, however, require careful study and a full discussion of the advantages and disadvantages of various alternative solutions. Such deliberation is most effective in small groups like committees.

The worship and liturgy committee, for example, could include two or three members of the official board and several members from the congregation at large. The leader can recruit members representing various ages, theological viewpoints, and any minority groups in the church. That way, when the liturgy of Sunday worship is changed by taking the offering after the sermon instead of before, many congregation members will recognize that their needs and desires were taken into account by their representatives on the committee before the decision was made. They also know there is a group that will listen to their reactions to such a change and consider them in the ongoing planning of worship.

Working through committees does more than simply build goodwill in the congregation through representative decision making. My own research indicates that members who feel they are heard on policy and program decisions of the church are likely to attend worship more frequently than those who do not feel so represented. Among seventy churches I surveyed in 1977, church attendance rose or fell in a statistically significant way based on how members felt about the adequacy of deliberation and the degree of participation in decision making in their churches. The wise leader will want to encourage worship attendance by assuring ample participation in decision making at the committee level.

Committee Meetings Are the Best Way to Insure That Work Will Get Done. Church work is a sideline for most volunteer workers in the church. It competes with occupations, family responsibilities, and recreational activities for time and attention. Therefore the principle of regular meetings is important to getting work done in the church. A monthly meeting of an ongoing program or administrative committee provides a convenient opportunity for the leader to communicate with the workers. The committee members who ordinarily work in specific programs or administrative areas get an opportunity to ask questions or get help——and everyone gets a regular reminder of what he or she is supposed to be doing.

If every member of the evangelism committee was assigned to make a personal visit to one or more than one family listed on a prospect card, the next monthly meeting becomes a deadline by which to make the call. On the other hand, the absence of a monthly meeting makes it easy to put off or forget one's duties. When the finance committee meets every month, the monthly treasurer's statement can be reviewed, bills can be approved for payment, and problems of accounting or interest accrued can be resolved as they arise. Furthermore, with the experience of monthly discussions about church income and expenses, the committee will be prepared to devise a responsible budget for the following year.

Committee work may not always be fun or exciting, but it continues to be the most effective way to get a large portion of the work of the church done by volunteers.

Setting Goals and Objectives for the Committee

In the awkward moment right after the first meeting is opened with prayer, everybody is sitting there just a little bit anxious, wondering how to get started. The best way to start a committee is to talk about where it should finish. The real question in everybody's mind is: "After we've been at this for a year, what difference will so many hours of meetings make? Will anything get done? How will we know whether it did or not?" The answer is to set goals and objectives for the coming year.

Planning for a year's committee work can be done in either of two ways. The chairperson can write up a set of goals and objectives and propose them to the committee for consideration at that first meeting. Or the committee can spend that first meeting figuring them out together. Setting goals is done in the first five steps of an eight-step planning process.

Step One: List the Responsibilities and Needs the Committee Is Charged to Fulfill. If there is a job description or a set of standing rules for the committee, this step goes easier. Be sure to include anything related to the committee's work that no other group in the church is doing. Also be open to the new ideas or "emerging needs" that have never presented themselves before.

Step Two: Arrange the List of Responsibilities in Order of Priority or Importance. There are always more responsibilities and needs than any one committee could achieve, even if they had the Army Corps of Engineers working for them. If you cannot do everything, at least concentrate on the tasks that seem most important. Just put a number one next to the responsibility or need that appears most important to everyone. Then number the next most important with a two and so on until everything is numbered.

Step Three: Describe the Desired End Result as a Goal for Each Responsibility. At the end of the year what will have happened or changed as a product of your committee's working on that responsibility or need? A well written goal will be stated in terms that are measurable. Describe it so that anybody could tell whether or not your work was achieved. Avoid abstract descriptions such as "a greater commitment to Jesus," or "spiritual growth," because you'll never be able to see a year later whether you did any good with those matters. Instead, plan a specific series of spiritual renewal meetings. That's a concrete result of work.

Step Four: Plan Out Action Steps to Get to the Goal. What will you as a committee have to do to accomplish the goal as you stated it? For your spiritual renewal meetings, dates have to be set; approval of the governing board granted; speakers invited; promotion and publicity planned and carried out; and a concrete evaluation made

Figure 4—The Planning Process

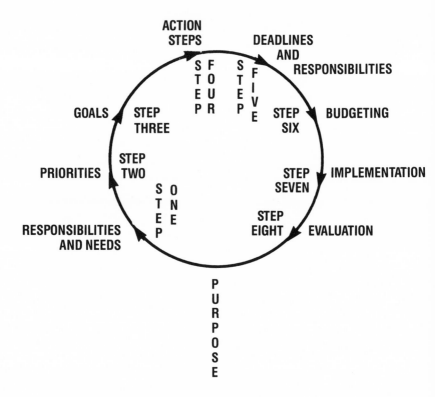

as to whether the meetings were successful or not. How many attendees do you expect? What kind of response do you want them to make?

Step Five: Set Deadlines for Each Action Step and Assign Responsibility for each activity to one or more members of the committee. With this step you will have planned the agenda of nearly every meeting for the year.

With the completion of these five steps, the committee has set its directions and agreed on desired end results. Now everyone will have a similar idea of what needs to get done and how everything ties together. Likewise, each committee member will have a degree of ownership in the committee's work because of his or her participation in this agenda. As a fringe benefit, setting goals and objectives is a useful tool for training the committee members in their responsibilities by giving them experience in working together as a committee. Finally, a written record of goals helps evaluate the committee's work at the end of the year, and becomes a starting place in setting goals for the following year. Figure 4 shows how the planning cycle fits together and points the way to the remaining three steps.

Step Six: Consider What It Will Cost to Carry Out the Planned Programs and Activities. This proposal is ordinarily passed on to the finance committee in time to plan the year's church budget.

Step Seven: Implement the Program. This is simply the committee carrying out the work it has planned.

Step Eight: Evaluate. At the end of the program year the committee examines its results in the light of the goals and objectives. Have they been attained? What might have been done better?

As the new program year dawns, the committee finds itself back at step one with its assigned purpose and is ready to reexamine responsibilities and needs.

Assigning Responsibilities

The business of assigning one or more members to take responsibility for a task or activity is so important it deserves a separate discussion. The single most common cause of work left undone in a church is failure to assign responsibility for a task. In its April meeting the Christian education committee agreed that prices would be obtained for a new videocassette recorder and a decision could be made on a purchase at the next meeting. When the minutes were read at the May meeting, everyone remembered the agreement. The Sunday school superintendent asked the chairperson what kind of prices had been found. The chairperson looked at the director of Christian education. No one had made the few phone calls necessary to have the information ready for a decision that night. Each person thought some other member would surely follow up on the task, but no one put those thoughts into words at the April meeting.

The situation brings to mind the fable of the mice who were starving because a prowling cat had come to live in their building. The cat kept sneaking up on them and preventing them from getting even a crumb from the kitchen. So the mice held a meeting to discuss the problem. After much debate, the oldest, wisest mouse suggested that a bell could be placed around the cat's neck so that it could no longer sneak up on them. Everyone cheered, and the group quickly voted in favor of the plan. The meeting was just about to break up when the youngest mouse spoke up. "I see just one little problem with the plan," she said. "Who is going to bell the cat?"

Next time your committee decides on a "perfect" plan for resolving a particular problem, be sure someone asks the key question—"Who is going to bell the cat?" Be sure also that someone agrees to take on the task.

Much of the New Testament teaching about getting the Lord's work done implies that such work is not to be done solo but in small groups. Jesus spoke of his presence among groups of two or three. When he himself had work to do, he took three disciples with him (healing Jairus' daughter, Mark 5:37; the transfiguration, Mark 9:2; in the garden, Mark 14:33). Further he sent his disciples out as missioners in pairs (Mark 6:7). I believe Jesus knew what we are learning afresh from the behavioral sciences, that small groups are an effective and valuable way to carry out the work for which we have been called. In every church may be found capable, committed people to serve together on committees or boards. By all means find them and appoint them!

4

Getting Work Done
with the Official Board

The apostles and elders held a meeting. . . after a long debate, Peter rose and addressed them. At that the whole company fell silent and listened to Barnabas and Paul. . . . When they had finished speaking, James summed up. . . . Then the apostles and elders, with the agreement of the whole church, resolved. . . .
—Acts 15:6,12,13,23

I know why they call it the board, Daddy," said an insightful eight-year-old. "Because the meetings are so boring!" In an action-oriented society, for people accustomed to fast-moving television entertainment, a group that sits for a long time to debate issues and make decisions sounds less than appealing. In my tradition, we call the official board the "session," which literally means "sitting." Other denominations have names like administrative board, consistory, deacons, parish council, and trustees. Whatever the label, a group of officers is responsible for the worship and work of the particular church. The origins of such groups date back to the council of elders in the synagogues of Jesus' time. The Christian movement of the first century adopted the same form, and we have the minutes of a very important meeting of the council of elders of "Old First Church" of Jerusalem in the fifteenth chapter of Acts. Through the ages the church in its many forms has reaffirmed its belief that decisions made by councils represent the moving of God's Holy Spirit to guide the church. We have also recognized that councils may err. Councils sometimes err by doing too much or going too far. More frequently, however, they err by not doing much of anything except talk. This chapter gives a few practical hints on helping board meetings move from faith to action.

Making an Agenda to Help Get Work Done

The traditional agenda for a board meeting looks something like this:

Call to Order
Opening Prayer
Reading of the Minutes
Treasurer's Report
Pastor's Report
Correspondence
Old Business
New Business
Adjournment

In my experience, this agenda usually hinders effective discussion and decision making. Two principles of group meetings offer an explanation of that failure:

1. The Principle of Available Energy. A well-known proverb describes the universal principle of energy in meetings: DEACONS DEBATE FROM SEVEN TO EIGHT.

When people come to a meeting, they want to dig into some meaty issues. Their energy level is high. That high energy lasts about an hour and then begins to drop. If the meeting began at seven o'clock, their minds will not grasp subtle differences nearly as well after eight. In the second hour decisions will be made that receive less than the full attention of the group. By the third hour, only sheer dedication and persistence keep a board on its task.

2. Sawyer's Law of Meetings: Matters brought up first in a meeting receive the greatest time and attention, whether they deserve them or not. This second principle is related to the first but goes a step further. Because of the available energy, groups have a tendency to talk longest and with greatest vigor about the first issue presented at the meeting. If the first item is whether to buy a five dollar wastebasket for the church lounge, there will be ample debate of the merits of metal versus wicker baskets, and probing questions about where the basket will be placed, who will empty it, what kinds of waste will be allowed to be placed in it, and whatever happened to that nice basket that Mrs. Jones bought for the church back in 1902? Such discussion appears to be a waste of the creative energy of the highest governing body of our beloved congregation. Yet, without realizing it is happening, groups seldom fail to fall into the trap described by "Sawyer's Law." After the available energy is drained away by discussing the trivia of reports and minutes and letters from denominational executives, and of wastebaskets (where some of the just mentioned reports frequently are filed), the board gets to the part of the agenda in which a decision must be made about offering a Bible study class for retarded persons. Is there any wonder that the ensuing discussion is fuzzy, lifeless, and prone to be postponed?

A flexible agenda is the answer to the problem. Throw the standard agenda in the new wastebasket and resolve to utilize the operating principles of human meetings. Whoever sets the agenda will then be free to schedule the most important, most complex, or even the most controversial issues during the first hour of the meeting. The big item on the agenda one month might be classified as "old business" or it might be presented in the treasurer's report. The first matter could be a bombshell dropped in a letter to the board from a member of the church, or it might be a new and urgent proposal from the building and grounds committee for a new boiler, since the old one just broke and the temperature will drop to freezing by next weekend.

By the same principles, matters that require board action, but are routine or relatively simple, can be scheduled for later in the meeting. Reports which give information to the board without requiring a decision can likewise be postponed until later in the meeting. By that point everyone will be glad to listen politely and not have to say or do anything.

Very controversial issues usually deserve to be placed early on the agenda. Discretion needs to be observed, however, about controversial issues by whoever prepares the agenda. If the presiding officer or pastor decides that an expected conflict surrounding the selection of colors for painting the rest rooms should not be encouraged, it could be intentionally placed late on the agenda. In the long-term values of the church and the kingdom of God, what difference will it make to paint the johns beige instead of green?

The method presented here of rearranging the agenda to fit the issues for each particular meeting could be labeled "manipulative." The label is accurate, for it is blatantly manipulative. It may be used for good or for less than honorable motives. A friend recently mentioned that, in his business, managers intentionally stack the agenda of meetings by placing issues of minor importance at the beginning and pet proposals at the end, when most participants will not care how the vote comes out. Such covert use of this method is not recommended. The method may be used openly, however, and be explained to the board without apology, exactly as it has been presented here. The board holds a check-and-balance option when it takes action to adopt the agenda at the beginning of the meeting. Any member of the board can, and should, override the judgments of the agenda-maker by moving an amendment which places an item at a different spot on the schedule. That way the decision about the agenda is ultimately up to the entire body rather than just one person.

This flexible agenda method has worked well in a number of settings. Credit for the concept is given to the Rev. D. Lorrin Kreider, of Columbus, Ohio, an outstanding pastor and administrator, from whom I learned it ten years ago.

Identifying items "For Action" or "For Information" is another method of helping the board get its work done by careful agenda making. Only three purposes exist for presenting an item to the official board: (1) the board is requested to take an action on the item; (2) the board needs to be informed about it; or (3) the presenter wishes to have the benefit of a discussion of an issue by the board without the board's taking action. Thus a presenter is asked to say at the beginning of a report whether the item coming before the board at this time is for action, information, or for discussion. With this signal the members of the board may prepare themselves to respond appropriately.

The reverse side of this procedure is also helpful. If a committee or officer has no business requiring the action of the board, and no information that the board particularly needs, the proper statement is "no report." Some officers fear they might appear unproductive if they bring no report to the board. Consequently the board is forced to endure such comments as:

My Christian Education Committee met with all members present on September 21. We had a very interesting discussion of the Halloween Party planned for the children next month by Alice and Donna. The new children's offering envelopes were passed around and everyone liked them.

> Plans for adult education programs for Winter Term are not quite completed now, but William expects to have them ready for us next month [and so on]. . . .

All of these matters are of value to the committee itself, but it can handle them on its own authority without the advice and consent of the board. Occasionally, officers need to be reminded that the statement "no report" officially means that the committee is working hard on its own business, and needs nothing from the board at this meeting.

An example of a printed agenda, prepared on the flexible approach, with items marked for action or information, is shown in Figure 5.

How Much Time Should Board Meetings Take?

When I first began serving in a pastorate, board meetings began at 7:30 p.m. and lasted to 10:00, and sometimes to 10:30 or 11:00. In refining the flexible agenda process with the board, and getting better acquainted with the officers and their committees, I was able to chip away at the length of those meetings. Today the board rarely meets for more than two hours. At first not even I believed the work could get done in two hours, but the officers and I together have found ways that work. We get the same amount of business done in less time. Marking items "action" or "information" helps. Giving early agenda times to the big items helps. Using the "action form" discussed later helps.

Another technique seems to help even more to keep the

Figure 5—The Flexible Agenda
Governing Board Agenda

December 8, 1986
Meeting in Church Library

I.	Call to order		7:00 P.M.
	Devotions and prayer		
II.	Approval of agenda, minutes, and roll	Action	7:10 P.M.
III.	Reports		
	A. Finance Committee		7:15 P.M.
	1. November financial statement	Inform	
	2. 1987 budget	Action	
	3. Preparation for annual meeting	Action	
	B. Evangelism Committee		7:40 P.M.
	1. Proposal on church photo directory	Action	
	2. Other business		
	C. Executive Committee		8:00 P.M.
	1. Memorial list purchases policy	Action	
	D. Personnel Committee		8:15 P.M.
	1. Removals from Board of Deacons	Action	
	2. Other work in progress	Inform	
	3. Nominations for General Assembly	Action	
	E. Property Committee		8:25 P.M.
	1. Requests for keys to building	Action	
	F. Stewardship committee		8:35 P.M.
	1. Proposal for Christmas offering	Action	
	2. Results of stewardship campaign	Inform	
	G. Christian Education Committee		8:40 P.M.
	1. Program plans	Inform	
	2. Request on library plaque	Action	
	H. Worship Committee		8:45 P.M.
	I. Pastor's report		8:50 P.M.
	J. Clerk's report		8:55 P.M.
	1. Correspondence	Inform	
	2. Death: L. T. Jones Nov. 29, 1986	Inform	
IV.	Miscellaneous Business		9:00 P.M.
V.	Adjournment	Action	9:05 P.M.

board on schedule. We print on the agenda the time each report is to begin. Just as we know in advance what items are coming to the board for action, we also have a feel from the committees as to how much time the items will require or how controversial they might be. Officers can glance at the agenda and recognize that the finance committee has some major items coming up because its report is placed first and has been given one-half hour for several items for action. The building and grounds committee, on the other hand, can be expected to have very little to report or no report because its placement on the agenda is last and it is given the routine minimum of five minutes. In the same way, the printed agenda gives a continuous sense of "how we're doing" on the schedule. If we are far behind, extraneous comments are kept to a minimum. If we are ahead, the group may take more time than allowed on a subject of common interest.

One of the difficulties in keeping meetings short is the phenomenon called "air time." Many officers believe, without realizing it, that their presence is validated if they have a chance to make two or three comments during the span of the meeting. They like to hear themselves talk and assume everyone else does as well. Some seem to want more air time than others. The job of the presiding officer is to allow a little air time to everyone who needs it without letting the schedule get out of hand. A helpful comment by the presiding officer might be, "Now is there anyone wishing to speak who has not been heard on this matter?" In training church officers, two suggestions pave the way for controlling air time. First, they are encouraged to speak up in the board meetings, because their participation is important. Second, they are asked to be sure their comments are relevant and have not been made by anyone else in the same discussion.

Finally, the length of the board meeting is inversely proportional to the effectiveness of committees. If a committee has considered an issue carefully and presents its case to the board as fully as possible, both confusion and discussion time are saved. With a history of committee competence, officers learn to trust each other's work and feel less need to rehash what the committee has already done.

How to Get a Motion Approved by the Board

A common difficulty in working with the official board is to get approval of something new or different in the life of the church. "They will never buy this one," people begin to think. A strange phenomenon affects some people when they become members of a board. They become cautious, conservative, even suspicious, because they are responsible for the spiritual and temporal business of God's special people. They feel pressure from the many constituencies of the congregation. They want to know the answers to all the possible questions before they act. This phenomenon is good in itself, but it can block progress.

The way to take advantage of this serious sense of responsibility is to anticipate as many of the possible questions about a proposal as you can in making a presentation. If you are not sure how to do that, the "Action Form" (Figure 6) is a helpful aid. When a proposal is presented in that format, the officers have everything before them in black and white. The presenter needs to make only a few general comments about the proposal and let the paper do the talking. An alternative is to have the format written up for yourself to read to them. Use of the Action Form works! It forces the committee to do its homework to bring in the best possible proposal, and it gives a sense of confidence and security to these stodgy old board members. One thing the Action Form will not do: It does not promise to make a basically bad idea look good.

Building the Board into a Team

All the discussion in this chapter has been aimed at getting work done by getting rid of the fluff, the extraneous confusion and distraction that floats around in the air in board meetings. Some people might imagine this is turning the board into a cold and efficient work machine which refuses to have fun. Nothing could be further from the truth. All of the agenda building and action techniques actually free the board from the burdens of spinning its wheels, and permit the group to become a team.

None of the task-oriented techniques work, however, without a sense of team spirit and solidarity. In the official board, as in leader-worker ties, relational needs have their place alongside task concerns. Effective groups learn how to keep the two in balance. The secret to building a good team is shared responsibility. Nearly everyone can play a role in keeping the group healthy and happy. Six relational roles, as identified by Malcolm and Hulda Knowles, have been widely taught in building a team:

Encouraging——Being friendly, warm, responsive to others; praising others and their ideas, agreeing with and accepting the contributions of others.

Mediating——Harmonizing, conciliating differences in points of view, making compromises.

Gate keeping——Trying to make it possible for another member to make a contribution by saying, "We haven't heard from Jim yet," or suggesting limited talking-time for everyone so that all will have a chance to be heard.

Standard setting——Expressing standards for the group to use in choosing its subject matter or procedures, rules of conduct, ethical values.

Following——Going along with the group, somewhat passively accepting the ideas of others, serving as an audience during group discussion; being a good listener.

Relieving tension——Draining off negative feeling by jesting or throwing oil on troubled water, diverting attention from unpleasant to pleasant matters. [12]

Taking time to talk about relational matters is important in building and maintaining team spirit on the board. A good exercise for introducing new board members to team building is to have them tell what name they want to be called by in the meetings, and why. Sometimes groups discover that the person everybody has been calling Jimmy for years really prefers to be known as James. Some boards plan to spend the last ten minutes of their meeting talking about their feelings from the meeting. Those few minutes can save time later if something unresolved can be

Figure 6—Action Form

1. Action requested (Motion stated in full):

2. Person or group initiating action

3. Date of request

   Date action to take effect

4. Need which this action addresses (Problem or concern):

5. How this action would meet the need

6. Expected cost
   Financial:

   Number of people and time:

7. Alternative solutions not recommended (Other possible actions, considered but rejected):

8. Disposition of action:
   Adopted _____   Referred _____   to whom _____

   Failed _____   Postponed _____   to time _____

   Amended as follows:

uncovered and dealt with right there. Work goes easier and faster when all members feel comfortable enough to tell one another what they think and feel about the task before them.

How would it have felt to attend the council meeting that day at First Church, Jerusalem, which is described in Acts 15? The debate took up the early part of the meeting with people speaking enthusiastically on both sides of the issue of circumcision for the Gentiles. After a while Peter gave his opinions and beliefs on the matter. Sometimes it is important for a leader to state his or her position clearly. Next on the docket the guests were invited to tell stories of their mission among the Gentiles. I can imagine the officers smiled and even laughed at some of the incidents, which also answered many of the questions the elders had about the matter before them. When it appeared that everything had been said, the presiding officer summarized the whole discussion and proposed a solution. A vote was taken and the resolution passed overwhelmingly. The group even remembered to assign two members to carry the decision to the Gentile churches. Everyone felt good about the meeting and about the decision. Your official board can get its work done in such a fashion, too.

5

Getting Work Done with the Pastor

Our leader, . . . or bishop, must be above reproach,
faithful to . . . one [spouse,] sober, temperate, courteous,
hospitable, and a good teacher. . . . Must be one
who manages his [or her] own household well. . . .
— *1 Timothy 3:2,4*

When people joked about his only working on Sundays, a pastor I know used to retort that he actually worked for the church full time during the week and donated his time to the church on Sundays! The way the pastor spends that time during the week, and the extent to which anything gets accomplished, depend heavily on the way the members interact with him or her as they work together in the church. In order to aim accurately at the ideal for pastoral character suggested to Timothy in the passage cited above, the pastor is going to need a lot of help. Anyone who knows, works with, lives with, or is a pastor can benefit from reflection on the ideas in this chapter.

Freeing the Pastor to Do Essential Work

The images of the pastor's role may be as diverse as the number of members in the congregation. Two images are common enough to highlight here and to describe the helpful and harmful elements in each concept.

Some churchgoers picture the pastor as the *employee* of the church. There is enough truth in this image to make it very popular. The congregation pays the salary, provides the benefits, and has a right to determine the working activities of the employee so paid. Some churches are so blatant in this attitude that ministers are often pulled apart as they try to please every demanding parishioner. Other churches, more sophisticated, make uniform demands through a governing board or personnel committee. Either way the message is clear: "We pay your salary, we call the shots." The "shots" could be called for tougher preaching or more lenient preaching, more formal liturgy or more modern worship, depending on the whim of those attempting to call them. Of course that's the problem with this image. A pastor is expected to provide guidance and leadership based on seven years of college and professional schooling and on experience. But it is contradictory to order someone to "lead" in a certain way. The pastor who is expected to follow orders has lost the freedom to carry out the essential work of ministerial leadership.

A pastor continues to be an employee of the church in one helpful sense. The church members do have a right to some accounting of the pastor's work. How the pastor spends professional time must be left to that pastor's discretion, but that time allocation should be reported regularly to the governing board for its information and comments. More about this reporting will be said under the heading of the pastor's workload later in this chapter. Whenever there is a disagreement over what the pastor is doing, the matter is open for discussion. Often misunderstandings can be overcome early in this accounting, either by the pastor's adjusting allocations in a way consistent with his or her own view of ministry or by a clear and persuasive explanation of why that way seems better for the present. Over a longer period of time, if a pastor and governing board continue to disagree about the pastor's work, a relocation might be in order. What I am proposing here is a distinction between subservience and accountability; only the latter can free a pastor to be a true leader.

Another popular image of the pastor's work is that of *staff or executive officer.* One way of interpreting this image is found in this notion that "staff does whatever the volunteers will not do." Under this image pastors frequently find themselves writing minutes of committee meetings, ordering supplies, recruiting volunteer workers, sweeping floors, and locking doors. None of these activities is inherently wrong for the pastor. The problem lies in the frequency of their occurrence. A practical problem with them is that the church is paying a relatively high dollar amount for such labor when it could be obtained at half that cost or for free. Ministers often fall into the same problem with this image. They want to be helpful. They like to see something tangible come from their work. They may even enjoy some kinds of activities and keep the "fun" all to themselves. However, consistent pastoral handling of routine tasks around the church is dangerous to the health of the church as well as the pastor. Church members are denied opportunities to serve while the pastor crowds his or her professional schedule with these chores. Sometimes people include such work by the pastor in the category of "administration," but a more accurate term might be "administrivia." The real role of an administrator is to help others serve.

The healthy church will encourage its pastor to spend most available time doing a unique job of spiritual guide, theologian, teacher. Free the pastor to mediate the essentials of ethical and religious truth to the congregation and to the community. Provide space and time for the integrity of the ministerial calling to yield its fruit. Recognize the pastor as a professional whose skill and training elicit respect. Not every church member will approve of every activity of the pastor, but each church member can recognize the pastor's right to follow his or her own conscience and wisdom in setting professional priorities.

The Pastor's Workload

In contrast to the little joke about only working on Sundays, most pastors work hard, spend long hours on their jobs, and have little time to give to themselves or their families. Clergy and their spouses have reported that time together is the most common difficulty their marriages face.[13] Because pastoral work is not routine–it cannot be reduced to doing the same tasks in the same ways at the same times in every workday or workweek–many clergy experience difficulty in budgeting, allocating, or limiting the time they spend in their professional activities. The pastor may say, "I feel I'm running all the time, from morning to night, seven days a week, and I cannot seem to get control of this job." As the old guy down at the general store used to say, "Customers keep coming in and interfering with business." There are interruptions, emergencies, telephone calls–not to mention stacks of letters, magazines, and books–vying for the pastor's attention.

In spite of the heavy workload, however, a pastor has a hard time explaining the job to members of the congregation. Furthermore, because of the call to serve God, it's hard to stop being a minister and go home. More and more studies are indicating that burnout and marriage difficulties are becoming increasing concerns for clergy. How, then, can the pastor be faithful to the portrayal in 1 Timothy 3, and at the same time maintain a balance of personal and family health?

"Never finished." A simple fact of church life is that, like the proverbial housewife, the minister's work is never done. Pastor Axel R. Rate rushes from hospital to nursing home to luncheon appointment to the study to an important committee meeting. No matter how fast Axel moves, there is always one more call he could have made, one other meeting he might have attended, and one more article or reference he should have checked before he could really call it quits. Copastors Dee Sently and Ann

Order have carefully structured their workweeks to plan adequate time for every essential activity, but they always find that their estimates of time were short and new demands crowded into the middle of their schedule. Axel, Dee, and Ann probably end each workweek exhausted and feeling guilty because they did not accomplish what they set out to do.

After several years of this kind of scheduling and struggling to achieve in the ministry, bad work habits set in and the indications of "workaholism" take over.[14] Part of the blame for these conditions comes from the expectations of the congregation and of the community, and usually there is little the pastor or the concerned church member can do to change them. Another significant source of the problems can be found located between the ears of the pastor, however. "Expect more of yourself because you are working for God!" clergy seem to say to themselves. This is wrong. If the compulsion to work without ceasing presents itself as a serious, consistent hindrance to effectiveness or to enjoyment of life, the pastor may need to seek professional counseling to understand and redefine the issues. I have found that a simple spiritual reminder helps me keep my job in perspective. Whenever I find myself feeling guilty over unfinished business, I tell myself: ONLY JESUS WAS ABLE TO SAY "IT IS FINISHED."

The Gospels show that Jesus declared his work complete shortly before his last breath on the cross. His work was the salvation of the world's population, which required his death by painful and humiliating execution.

Orthodox Christian teaching has held that his death was a once-and-for-all event. As a pastor I was called to carry the message of Jesus' death and resurrection using my limited gifts and time. Death by overwork is not required of me. Indeed, for me to assume the role of Savior and expect to be able to finish my work is *to pretend* I am God. Whenever I recall this truth, I find I am better able to concentrate on accepting my own limitations, and to go home seeking rest and refreshment, willing to leave the work for another day.

Priorities and Posteriorities. In planning work and allocating time most people have learned how to set priorities. The procedure is simple enough:

1. List all of the tasks or projects that are needed.
2. Rearrange the list so that the most important or most urgently needed task or project is first and the others are listed in descending rank from most to least urgent.
3. Address the tasks in the order listed.

The items at the top of the list are called "priorities" because they rank ahead of the others. Nearly everyone recognizes the need to work on high-priority tasks.

Often, however, zealous workers in the church (and in other organizations) forget that when you identify priorities, you also relegate items to the bottom of the list, which are called "posteriorities." If time, money, and personnel are insufficient to carry out all items on the list, logic would suggest that the items on the bottom will simply not get done. Some of the posteriorities can be reentered on the list for the next week or month or year and again ranked in order of urgency. Others can be delegated to lay members. Finally, though, there are some items on the busy pastor's list that may never get done. The best attitude is to release them gracefully as the "fish that got away." Adopting the method of setting priorities and posteriorities can be a tremendous assist in managing the pastor's workload.

Allocating Professional Time Through "Modules." After the pastor has accepted the element of decision in choosing tasks and projects, the next step is relatively easy. Each pastor can intentionally choose how much time to allocate for working and when that time shall be spent. Begin taking control of pastoral time by drawing a simple grid on a sheet of paper, as shown in Figure 7. The grid represents a week. There are twenty-one modules of time in the week with a morning, an afternoon, and an evening for every day.

Figure 7—The Pastor's Week

Sun	Mon	Tues	Wed	Thur	Fri	Sat	
X	X	X	X	X	X		Morning
	X	X	X	X	X		Afternoon
	X		X	X			Evening

The pastor can choose how many modules are needed to do the job desired. A regular five-day work week would total ten modules. A six-day work week would add up to twelve. Each evening spent in church work, whether in meetings, in visitation, or in study, is an additional module. A pastor in a medium-sized church of average complexity might decide, for example, to aim for a fourteen-module work week as the norm. The average work week for that pastor might look like the grid in the figure above.

> 5 mornings during the week
> 5 afternoons
> 1 Sunday morning
> 3 evenings
> ―――
> 14 modules of work for the week

Such a schedule would allow one full day off on a normal week.

On those not-so-rare occasions in which work is scheduled for four, five, or even six evenings in the week, or for church responsibilities on the regular day off, an advance look at the coming week's grid alerts the pastor that the module norm will be exceeded. Then the pastor can choose a morning, afternoon, or both to "take off" for home, family, or recreation in that same week or in a week shortly following. This becomes a balancing act, not unlike balancing a budget of limited dollars.

Many harried clergy look at the module system and shake their heads in unbelief. They cannot imagine that they can control their time so neatly. They wonder how they could ever get enough work done in a limited amount of time to meet their own and others' expectations. The common experience of pastors who have tried the system over a period of time, however, is that with a proper balance of work and time off, they begin to feel more rested and refreshed. As a result, they get as much work done in the time allotted as they previously did when they followed no self-discipline in allocating time. A physically, emotionally, and spiritually tired pastor is less efficient and less effective. It takes, for example, twice as long to write a sermon when the writer is exhausted as when a healthy balance of work and rest has been maintained.

One further advantage of the module system should be noted here. It is easy to explain and interpret to the personnel committee or governing board. A monthly record of the four weekly grids provides quick and easily recognizable accounting of how the pastor spends professional time. The grid report can be combined with a brief statistical report of the number of hospital calls, home visits, counseling sessions, church meetings, weddings, funerals, classes taught, and so forth, for the month. The introduction of the module system can become an opportunity to contract with the board on the amount of time mutually satisfactory. Furthermore, the monthly reporting can also provide an opportunity for the group to make helpful comments or critiques on the pastor's work in general. In the long run the module system of allocating time can be a conflict-reducing device by providing clear interpretation of the pastor's work and opportunity to discuss such matters in a spirit of openness.

A warning needs to be issued here, however. Inside each pastor's head is a little beeper that goes off at any suggestion of doing something for himself or herself. Taking a morning, an evening, or even a whole day for family or for recreation seems somehow sacrilegious. After all, a call to ministry demands a total commitment to help and serve others. Wayne Oates' beautiful book, *Confessions of a Workaholic,* suggests a creative way to circumvent the little guilt-beeper.[15] We usually assume it is the pastor's duty to be a good role model of the Christian life to the members of the congregation. If the pastor models workaholism—constant work under pressure with no time for self or family—church members will subtly receive the message that such devotion to vocation is the ideal. On the other hand, the pastor can convey by deed and interpret verbally that the responsibilities of spouse and parent are important in one's calling as a Christian. Marriage and parenthood are vocations, too, and family solidarity as a value is being sorely tested in the present culture. A wise church member can help the pastor get more work done and also be a better family member by gently recommending that the human needs of the pastor be recognized. Then, if all else fails, "throw the Book" at the pastor. Haul out 1 Timothy 3, where it says that the pastor must be one who manages well his or her own household. The manager who is never home cannot meet this standard.

Sooner or later most ministers are forced by their health, their domestic problems, or their career frustrations to recognize they are human, frail, limited in their ability to solve the problems of the world. In such a crisis the hints for workload management suggested here are proven aids.

Care and Feeding of the Pastor

In the secular workplace someone is usually assigned to oversee the worker's well-being. Perhaps it is the boss, the union, or the personnel officer. In many professions peer oversight fills this purpose to some degree. Somehow, though, the clergy have missed out on this benefit. Few denominations do an adequate job of supervision and nurturing their clergy. Ministers seldom turn to each other for help with job-related issues. And in only rare situations are church members wise and courageous enough to provide appropriate assistance to a minister. Just as rarely are the clergy aware enough of their needs to ask for the kind of help they really need. A large proportion of clergy problems would be eliminated if the minister or a wise church member would implement two simple techniques for the care and feeding of the pastor.

In the play *No Exit* Jean-Paul Sartre places his three characters in a room with no mirrors. The only way to see themselves is through each other's eyes. Life in the world is like that. Humans need other people to let them know how they are doing. If a church is organized into committees, one of them should be designated the personnel committee or pastoral relations committee. Lacking this, a small group of members who represent a knowledgeable cross section of the congregation can serve less formally as a minister's support group. These people have two tasks: First, they provide the pastor with feedback on how things are going. Second, they can review the adequacy of the pastor's compensation package.

Evaluation by Encouragement. At least once a year this group is called together to meet with the pastor to evaluate his or her work. Ministers and church members usually approach such meetings with more than a little fear, because evaluation is hard to give and harder to receive. With a rule that all criticism will be constructive, the fears are greatly reduced. The purpose of the evaluation, after all, is to help the pastor do a better job, and to improve the "goodness of fit" between pastoral and congregational expectations. The evaluation is done in the spirit of the apostle Paul's words, "And I will show you a still more excellent way" (1 Corinthians 12:13). Church members and pastor are partners in a joint ministry and mission, and each has a stake in the other's performance.

Prior to the time when the pastor meets with the committee, the pastor and chairperson might want to agree on an outline of the areas for discussion. Committee members may be encouraged to do some homework by reflecting on these areas, and even by informally checking with other members about their perceptions of the pastor's work. At the meeting itself, the pastor or the chair can review the purpose of the meeting. A covenant of confidentiality is helpful in this situation, so that both pastor and members feel free to share personal feelings. The meeting should always be held with the pastor present.

An example of the areas of discussion for the evaluation meeting is found in materials provided by the Presbyterian Church.[16] Eight pastoral roles are suggested, with description in each role of what the competent pastor does.

1. Director of worship
2. Facilitator of pastoral care
3. Leader and interpreter of mission
4. Coordinator of church education
5. Facilitator of parish/community relationships
6. Administrator
7. Participator in denominational government
8. Member of the Profession

No single pastor will be highly competent in all eight areas. Strengths and limitations will be identified in the list, as the committee discusses the areas with the pastor. An attitude of grace will be more likely to produce satisfactory change than an attitude of judgment.

An alternative to this approach would be for the pastor to present to the personnel committee a list of goals for the year to come. As discussed in Chapter 3, goals are best stated in measurable terms. The pastor should not be afraid to include deadlines and numbers in the statements. The committee may want to suggest clarification or even modification of some goals based on its perceptions of the congregation's needs. At the end of that year the committee meets with the pastor to review the goals and their accomplishment. If a goal was not achieved, why not? Was it too high a goal? Were there extenuating circumstances? Was the pastor simply not working toward its achievement? Were the time lines too short? Should the goal be renewed for next year, or should it be modified or dropped? What can the committee or other church members do to assist the pastor in meeting this goal in the future?

A note of caution about the evaluation process concludes this discussion. Both pastor and members need to be clear as to the positive, constructive nature of the evaluation. The committee's role is to help; it is to hold a mirror to the pastor's effectiveness in church work, not to crack a whip. The objective is to prevent conflict rather than create it. When conflict does erupt in this process, a neighboring pastor or a denominational consultant may be invited to meet with the committee and pastor, to head off further erosion of the relationship.

Setting the Pastor's Salary. Historically, one of the least effective areas of church work has been setting the pastor's salary. Few church members know anything about their pastor's compensation and fewer know how to discuss the matter reasonably with the pastor. Similarly, few ministers wish to make requests of their church in financial matters, and those who want to, do not know how to make the overtures constructively.

The discussion of the pastor's salary should begin with the personnel committee or other support group. The task is best not left to the finance committee or the trustees, because such groups are conditioned to think primarily of the financial condition of the church, instead of its spiritual and programmatic well-being. The members of the personnel committee have built a relationship with the pastor through the evaluation process and are better acquainted with the work load and pressures of the pastor. They are more likely to realize that fair treatment in financial matters will assist the pastor in getting work done.

When the committee meets with the pastor to review the adequacy of the salary, several guidelines are helpful:

1. A full picture of the compensation package must be given. Consider not only the cash salary but also housing, utilities, use of car for church business, continuing education and book costs, pensions and medical insurance, and special tax benefits and liabilities of clergy. Be very clear that when comparing the pastor's salary with that of others in the community, only the cash salary and housing values are compared. Most people when they think about how much they make do not consider fringe benefits and reimbursed expenses as part of their "salary."

2. The responsibility of the church is to provide enough financial compensation to "free the pastor from worldly cares." If the family in the parsonage is constantly worried about meeting basic expenses because of inadequate compensation, the pastor is not able to devote full energy to the work of ministry!

3. Ministers are human and respond to concrete expressions of appreciation. A raise or a bonus beyond the basic

cost of living is likely to be a good motivator for pastoral work for the church.

4. Study of articles or books on clergy compensation such as Manfred Holck's articles in *The Clergy Journal* (P.O. Box 1625, Austin, TX 78767) can help a committee understand the current issues of clergy compensation.

5. The committee will find help from denominational guidelines for clergy compensation. The pastor's salary can be compared with those of pastors in churches of comparable size in the denomination. Comparisons can also be made with the standards for teachers and administrators in the public schools of the community. At the very least, no pastor should be paid less than the average salary of members of the church board, who are the pastor's closest partners in ministry.

6. Both the pastor and the committee will bring to this meeting proposals for the compensation package for the coming year. Then in face to face conversation they can compare proposals, discuss the relative feasibility of each, and come to understand the reasons for any significant differences between them. The conversation should seek compromises where that is possible. Ideally the pastor and committee will reach an agreement on a compensation package before it is sent to the governing board of congregation for approval.

For the church and pastor unaccustomed to this kind of dialogue over financial matters, the first year or two will seem awkward. But consistent use of the personnel committee for this purpose will eventually develop a healthy tradition and provide for overall better satisfaction with the compensation package by pastor and congregation alike. Any pastor who is unwilling to be assertive about money may just deserve the salary that results. And any congregation unwilling to enter into open conversations on the subject should not be too surprised to find their pastor moving on to another church just to get a raise.

The care and feeding of a pastor is a joint responsibility of the pastor and the congregation. Together they are seeking to provide the church with the leadership it needs for mission. Among the practical suggestions for leadership offered by the apostle Paul are these words about compensation: "Elders who do well as leaders should be reckoned worthy of a double stipend, in particular those who labour at preaching and teaching. For Scripture says, 'A threshing ox shall not be muzzled'; and besides, 'the worker earns his pay' "(1 Timothy 5:17-18, New English Bible).

This chapter is written with a sense of love and concern for pastors and for their churches. These suggestions are offered with a hope that loyal church members will implement some of them to provide their pastor with the best possible working conditions.

6

Getting Work Done in Communication

"Did not our hearts burn
within us while he talked . . . ?"
—Luke 24:32 (RSV)

From the creation story through the New Testament, the Judeo-Christian tradition has elevated talk to the highest level of respect. "And God said," is the beginning of all being. Jesus is called the "Word of God." And the risen Lord made conversation itself the "burning bush" of divine revelation on the road to Emmaus in Luke 24:32. The Reformers bowed to this wisdom when they placed the sermon at the center of their liturgies. In our time churches have rediscovered communication through the human relations movement and the insights of the behavioral sciences. This chapter is designed to apply both theological and organizational knowledge to getting work done in the church in communication.

What Is Communication

Communication is basic to human activity. When troubles arise in work or leisure, we are quick to blame them on communication. Unfortunately, however, diagnosis is easier than treatment, for we are too close to the problem to deal with it readily. Not only do we miss the forest because of the trees; we *are* the trees. As the comic strip character Pogo used to say, "I is met the enemy and they is us."

The following definition of communication can help break the process down to see it more clearly:

> COMMUNICATION is the expression of, perception of, and discriminative response to meaningful language and gestures.

The first observation of this definition is that it describes an ongoing series of events among people. A sentence spoken, a memo written, or a sign posted does not by itself constitute communication any more than the sound of the philosophical tree falling in the forest when no one is around. Anyone who refers to a letter or a memo as "my communication to you on this date" is missing the reality of communication. By the same token, using the term in the plural, "communication*s*," is inaccurate because the process involves continuing interaction rather than separate and identifiable acts or events.

Meaningful language and gestures are the exchangeable commodities used in the process of communication. Obviously the language and the gestures, to be meaningful, need to be commonly recognized by all the partners in the process. If you and I do not speak the same language, our words are meaningless to each other. For example the word "chat" may mean "informal conversation" to you and "a feline pet" to a French-speaking listener. Or, if you grew up in the same region of the Midwest as I did, the word might denote a very fine gravel used on roadways. While language can be ambiguous, it is more reliable in communication than gestures. Although much has been written about "nonverbal" communication in recent years, we still have not reached universal agreement about what most gestures mean. When I scratch my head do you assume I am expressing ignorance or a feeling of inferiority? For communication to be effective, the language and the gestures must be mutually meaningful.

There are three steps in effective communication:

1. *Expression* is the initiating action. This word implies an intentionality in speaking or moving on the part of the initiator of the communication process. If a student waves away a fly during a lecture, and the teacher responds to the upraised hand by calling on the student, true communication has not occurred because the student did not intend to express a desire to speak. When someone says, "It certainly is hot in here," and expects some kind of reply from someone else in the room, the expression has initiated a communicative process.

2. *Perception* is the second movement in the process; in it, someone else sees, hears, or feels the words or gestures expressed. The words "It certainly is hot in here" may not be perceived by anyone else because they were not

expressed loudly enough, or because no one was paying attention.

3. *Discriminative response* is the third movement in the process of communication. Someone speaks or acts in a way that indicates the expression was perceived accurately. Several discriminative responses are possible to "It certainly is hot in here." Someone might simply nod in agreement, get up and open a window, bring the expresser a glass of cold water, or even disagree that it seemed rather chilly instead. A comment at this point on the progress of a baseball game, however, probably would not qualify as a discriminative response. If the expresser really hoped to receive a glass of water in response to the comment, and a window was opened instead, further clarifying expressions would be needed (see Figure 8).

The Glue of the Organization. In the introduction to this book, an organization was interpreted as a system which could also be called a dynamically ordered whole. Human organizations such as clubs, businesses, and churches can be unbelievably complex in the way they work. Sometimes work gets done efficiently and effectively in them, and sometimes it does not. One fact is indisputable: Without communication, organizations fall apart. In the past four decades many methods have been proposed to improve communication in organizations from the simple "Don't say it, write it!" to the so-called secret of Japanese productivity—"Theory Z." Every theory of management has assumed that communication is the glue of the organization.

Figure 8—Stages in Communication

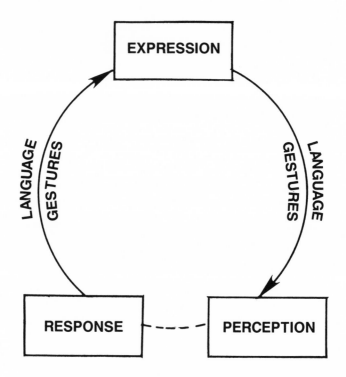

For anyone who does not grasp this fact, a simple experiment will bring the point into sharp focus. For a short period of time, establish a rule that all active workers in your church are forbidden to talk directly to each other about their church work. All information is to be shared with only one leader—who could be the pastor, the moderator of the congregation, the church secretary, or even "the best communicator" in the group. During the course of the experiment, the designated communicator bears the responsibility of conveying all necessary information to the people who need it. This person may speak to anyone he or she chooses, and anyone may talk to the communicator about church matters as often as necessary——but not to anybody else. To the extent the central actor in this experiment is able to carry the entire load of communication and share it fully, the organization will work effectively. Wherever the communicator fails to convey information or attitudes, work will falter and the organization will become ineffective. This experiment does not cut off the process of communication, but it channels it so restrictively that the glue is concentrated in one location. If it does not bond well there, the result is disorganization. Obviously it is best to spread the glue around so it will bond at as many points as possible.

"I-Witness" Messages

The most helpful way of getting good communication in a church is to be sure the organizational glue is of the best quality available. Two ingredients can be improved with moderate effort. The first improvement can be made with the expresser. The term "I-witness" is a way of teaching expressers to allow their words and gestures to reflect their own intentions, feelings, and ideas accurately. In one-to-one or small-group communication, accuracy of perception and response improves vastly when the expresser uses "I-witness" language instead of "you" language.

The message belongs to the expresser is the reason for the use of I-witness expressions. W. Burney Overton, of Atlanta, has successfully taught and counseled hundreds of church people with this principle of relational communication. The concept turns upside down our natural ideas about communication. We assume that words convey meaning mainly about the objects or events to which they refer. When I say, "The Tuesday evening Bible study class is an outstanding program," I think about what those words convey about the program itself. Actually, however, I am revealing as much about myself as I am about the Bible class. I am telling more about my values, my enthusiasm, my personal need for study and inspiration, my loyalty to a group or a teacher, or my own desire to promote the class, than about the class itself. Someone else may say "The Tuesday evening Bible class is a total waste of time." Logically, both statements cannot be true as descriptions of the class, but each may be true in the sense that they reveal the expresser. The message belongs to the expresser.

Once Overton's principle is recognized as a primary fact in communication, the next step is to clean up the expressions to reflect accurately the reality being revealed. A clearer way to talk about the Bible class is to turn the statement into an I-witness account. Say what is experienced, what is felt, what has happened. "*I have found* the Tuesday evening Bible class very helpful *to me* in my own religious searching." The negative statement might have been "The Tuesday evening Bible class has been a total waste of time *for me* because the members are studying material that *I studied* and mastered earlier in my life." As the Indian maiden said, "Speak for yourself, John."

I-witness expressions make it more likely that the hearer will perceive the meaning accurately and respond discerningly. If the perceiver of the expression is the teacher of the famous Tuesday Bible class, the statements in their original form might contribute either to a "big head" or to discouragement. The clearer I-witness expressions give helpful information about the expresser and need not imply that the problem is the teacher's.

Try a little training experience on this principle:

1. Think of something important you want to say to another member of your church.
2. Write out a statement as you initially consider it, without being very careful about the wording.
3. Read your statement and evaluate the extent to which it reveals clearly your own values, feelings, experiences, and ideas.
4. Rewrite the statement as an I-witness expression which clearly belongs to you. Use the first person singular in every possible way.

5. Imagine how the expression might be perceived and how the perceiver might respond. Consider how you would like the perceiver to respond.
6. One more rewrite might be necessary to improve the likelihood of a desired response from your perceiver.
7. Finally, initiate a communication process with the other person using your improved expression and observe what happens.

Your perceiver may or may not respond adequately to your expression because few people are accustomed to such clarity. To illustrate this variable, I did an experiment with a group of college students at a major university. All of them were in my class on interpersonal communication and had been present for lectures and discussion on the principle "The message belongs to the expresser." I sat with each of them individually in a room, with expert observers on hand, as I reviewed the concept of messages belonging to the expresser. Then I made a statement concerning *my* observations and attitudes about that particular student who was seated in front of me. Three out of four of them perceived the statement as a comment *about themselves,* despite the priming that should have prepared them to hear me talking about myself. The experiment gives important clues about how conditioned we are to unclear expressions, and how hard it is to retrain people to improve their communication skills.

Letting Our Words Be Christ's Words. These communication techniques work not only in the church but also at home or in the secular workplace. I-witness has special meaning in the church because of its application to the major mission of the church: evangelism. The fully committed Christian seeks to witness to Jesus Christ in every word and in every gesture. Certainly we all fall short of that ideal. Nevertheless, improving our communication skills will also improve our witnessing. The style of evangelism with which I have come to feel most comfortable is personal storytelling. I tell someone else about my own journey in life, and how God's love and care have sustained me. I talk about my own struggles with sin and suffering. I avoid telling people what they ought to do, or giving them frightening predictions about their lives without God. My own I-witness has been a helpful approach for many people I have met.

Jesus claimed his words were not his own but those of the one who sent him (John 7:16-18). The final goal of I-witness is that I can become so transparent in talking about myself that the Holy Spirit can use my words as her own in expressing important truths to others. In speaking of myself I do not seek my own glory, for I know there is no glory on my own. I hope that the glory will belong to God in my communication.

Listen and Say It Back

The second approach to improving communication in a church is enhancing the skills of perceivers. Frequently someone asks, "Does Jack know he is supposed to . . . ?" An appropriate answer might be, "I am not sure he knows, but I can assure you that he has been told." What goes on in the mind of a perceiver of a message is like the working of a black box to all but that person. Training to develop listening and response is a useful way to enrich the communicative activities in your church.

Improving listening skills can be quite simple. Every time someone makes a statement, let someone else say it back. This would make communication 100 percent better. Misunderstandings would be cut to a minimum, and both productive work and a happy climate would result. Unfortunately most of us balk at such a simple device. It sounds so contrived to put someone's statement in other words every time! Our culture does not encourage such clarity.

Here is an example of how we usually do it.

Example 1

E: Please have the minutes distributed to the church council by Tuesday.

P: But you know I cannot type! How can I get it done that quickly?

In this example we see misunderstanding from the outset. The perceiver thinks the expresser is saying: "You must type and duplicate the minutes and hand them to each council member by Tuesday." Instead of confirming that perception by checking it with the expresser, the perceiver reacts in a hostile manner. The method of "listen and say it back" demonstrated in Example 2 would diminish the misunderstanding.

Example 2

E: Please have the minutes distributed to the church council by Tuesday.

P: I am hearing you ask me to type, duplicate, and hand deliver the minutes by next Tuesday. Am I hearing you correctly?

E: No, I want you to turn in your handwritten version of the minutes to the secretary, in time for her to type them and mail copies to the council by next Tuesday.

P: So you want me simply to put my notes in clear hand-written form and bring them to the secretary who can type and distribute them by Tuesday. Is that what you are saying?

E: That is correct.

Example 2 shows how simple factual misunderstanding is avoided and work done more efficiently.

Example 3

E: I can't believe Alex did not turn in those minutes in time. This is a real mess.

P: I'm hearing you say you are angry at Alex because the minutes were not turned in. Is that correct?

E: Well, yes, I'm angry. But not so much at Alex as I am at the council for scheduling a meeting so quickly.

P: So your anger is more directed at the situation the council has put us in. Is that correct?

E: Yes. Thanks for giving me a chance to talk about this. It helps to get it out in the open.

In example 3 the issue is identification of feelings included in the message. We do not always say exactly how we feel, and emotions can get in the way of clear thinking and effective action if they are not dealt with appropriately. The perceiver in this example took some responsibility to go behind the bare information and try to identify the feelings that were involved in the situation. The first attempt to say it back labeled the feeling properly but did not have its object identified correctly. Further dialogue was required to get it clearly stated and understood.

Here are some guidelines for using the "listen and say it back" technique:

- Before reacting to a statement, restate it in your own words.
- Try to identify the real information and the underlying emotions in the expression.
- End the restatement with a question for confirmation—"Am I hearing you correctly?"
- Continue to say it back until the expresser agrees that the perceiver has heard correctly.
- Finally the perceiver reacts or responds to the statement with a statement or an action, if one is required.

Without a doubt this method seems stiff and awkward to anyone who is not used to it, but with practice it becomes more natural. The more it is used, communication will be clearer and more satisfying both for the perceiver and the expresser. This device has been the stock in trade of counselors for years. Even persons who are fully aware of the method and know that it is being used with them usually appreciate the effort to be understood. Listening is loving.

The Two-Way Street

Most of the contents of this chapter are so obvious that one wonders whether they need to be repeated. The final point of this chapter is another such self-evident truth that bears reiteration. We know that communication in a healthy organization is always a two-way street.

In normal, ongoing communicational activity, expresser alternately becomes perceiver and perceiver turns into expresser. Even the crudest conversation follows this pattern as one person tells a story and the other responds by saying, "You think you've got it bad; let me tell you what happened to me!" Sometimes we hear someone say, "I've been doing all the talking. Now tell me about yourself." Common sense aside, many churches have been hampered by a failure in two-way communication. Clergy and officers are anointed by tradition with authority that has often been used as a license to tell without listening. Traditional organizational principles have reinforced that tendency by defining communication as from the top down. But the church as a voluntary organization in the modern world no longer works well that way. Leaders gain the respect of followers by respecting them. Authority is granted to officers by the permission of the membership, who expect to be heard and appreciated.

Some types of glue require application to both of the surfaces that are to be bonded together. Such is communication. The organization is strengthened when participants express themselves clearly as I-witnesses and apply all their empathy to listening and responding.

7

Getting Work Done in the Midst of Conflict

"My aim is not my own will, but the will of [the one] who sent me."

—John 5:30

Tempers had flared and friendships were strained. The governing board thought they might have to fire the pastor because members were so unable to work with him. Outside consultants were invited by the pastor and the board to help resolve the conflict. During the third meeting of the involved parties, the pastor turned to one of the women who was the most vocal and asked her what was upsetting her the most. She responded candidly that, when the recent remodeling of the church was completed, new locks were installed on some of the doors, and the officers of the women's organization were no longer able to get into the kitchen. The pastor immediately left the room. When he returned a few minutes later, he handed a kitchen key to the woman who had identified the underlying issue in the conflict. The group instantly dissolved into laughter of relief, and the task of the consultants was completed.

Conflict Is Inevitable

The scene is not uncommon. Nearly every church has had conflict of lesser or greater degree in its recent history. Although the church holds the ideal of everyone seeking the will of God, the ambiguity of knowing exactly what that will is can bring sincere Christians into conflict with each other. The trustees may disagree with the deacons over an expenditure for the building. One women's circle may differ with another over the dates and themes of important programs. Furthermore, Christians vary in their reaction to conflict. Some react with shame and wish to avoid any appearance of unpleasant feelings. Others, expecting the conflict to be destructive, either leave the scene or jump into the fray with a martyr's zeal. Still others see it as a normal outlet for clearing the air.

The experience of organization theorists in business and industry can be helpful in this quandary. They have found three basic attitudes toward conflict:

Conflict is inevitable but agreement not possible
Conflict is avoidable, yet agreement not possible
Conflict is inevitable and agreement is possible. [17]

Organizations whose leaders affirm the last belief have been described as healthier than those headed by people holding the first two beliefs. The consultants involved in the "kitchen key" case described in the opening of this chapter entered the church with the belief that they were encountering an inevitable, though unpleasant, reality in the life of a congregation. Therefore they encouraged constructive engagement of the opposing parties. An expectation that the conflict could be eventually resolved aided the injured members in stating their feelings clearly to each other.

The second belief, that conflict is avoidable, promotes the saving-up of resentments and minor aggravations until they are so overpowering that the addition of one more trivial slight or difference provokes an outburst of conflict far greater than anyone expects. From their vast experience of consultation with churches, Speed Leas and Paul Kittlaus have pointed out: "The problem is that there is a big assumption inscribed in the folklore of the church that anger, hostile feelings, conflict, and differences of opinion are signs of sickness, selfishness, and failure in a church."[18] The fact that the church is an organization of human beings helps put these assumptions in perspective. Christians disagree, and conflict is therefore inevitable, but agreement is possible.

Now that we recognize the inevitability of conflict, the next question is: "Why are church conflicts so intense?" Men and women who are paragons of moderation on their jobs or in their social gatherings have been known to become passionate advocates or radical protesters in their churches. The explanation for this transformation may be found in the very nature of the church as an organization whose goal is the growth or expansion of a central religious value. Religion resides at the very core of who a person is and what a person wants to be. In traditional language, church has to do with one's personal salvation. Existentially, the church expresses the ultimate meaning or concern of a person's life. Any challenge to elements of one's church life becomes a threat to the very heart of that person's identity. Thus objectivity and reason are more easily abandoned in favor of emotional reaction. To tell a person that he or she may no longer sit in a favorite pew (often the one in the very back of the sanctuary) disturbs meaningful patterns of worship that may have sustained that individual through crises in the past. The unspoken reaction may be: "That is where I meet God every Sunday." People's personal investments in church life are considerably higher than for other activities in life. As a result the emotional temperature of church conflicts is proportionally higher.

Conflict Need Not Be Destructive

Someone who has experienced only those church fights that were bitter and destructive is likely to discount the optimism in this chapter. These concepts are not only theoretically sound, however, but I have field-tested them. There have been times in fifteen years of ministry when I entertained grave doubts about the constructive potential of conflict, but let me tell the stories of two actual events which confirm for me the validity of the approach presented here.

It was one of those very lean years for the church. The current year's budget was going to end up with a deficit, and the pledges for the coming year were inadequate to maintain the existing standards of program and staffing. With those prospects the chairs of various committees met on a cold and dreary December evening to cut the budget. It promised to be the kind of meeting in which the appropriate dress might be a helmet and flak jacket. Cherished programs would be called into question. The building operations people and the financial experts would argue for the wisdom of keeping up the property and letting programs go. There would be differences over mission contributions beyond the local church. Friends of various staff members would want to protect their turf.

As head of staff I prepared for the meeting as carefully as I could, and encouraged every other participant to do the same. After opening the meeting with prayer, I offered some rules for "fighting clean in the church" (see page 94). What followed met all our expectations for difficulty. Hard questions were posed, and painful decisions made. Nevertheless, none of the destructive elements we had feared were present. Obeying the proposed rules, members were emotional about their concerns, but remained considerate. People listened to each other. Through compromise the concerns for mission, human programs and property each ended up with more than their advocates had feared. New solutions to years-old problems were proposed. Everyone left the meeting with a sense of satisfaction that the church would continue to function at a high level due to the accomplishments of the evening. Agreement had been reached in the midst of conflict.

The second experience also had the potential for destructive conflict. A proposal came before our church governing board to build a ramp which would provide access to the sanctuary for handicapped people. The issue polarized the board. On one side were members who felt an obligation to open our building to people barred by its architecture. They favored spending church money on the project because they saw the church as a caregiver for the less fortunate. In the other camp were officers who feared the project would detract from the beauty of the building, who believed the actual number of people who would use such a ramp was too small to justify the expenditure, and who further preferred to have the money held in trust for future needs.

The proposal was discussed at one board meeting and the vote postponed to the next meeting to give ample time for reflection. At the second meeting opponents to the proposal requested that the issue be referred to the congregation for a decision. The "pro-ramp" members suspected this might be an attempt to defeat the issue, and at first they resisted the request. However they were finally persuaded of the fairness of such a referral.

The date was set for an open congregational meeting. The church newsletter published brief descriptions of the proposal and fair summaries of the two sides of the argument. At the congregational meeting, the debate was warm but not bitter. Fears were openly expressed. Respect for viewpoints was maintained, and members appeared willing to accept whatever decision the majority might make. Finally, just before the vote, one of the strong opponents of the ramp suggested a further condition that the project include a remodeling, at extra cost, of the room where the ramp would enter. That amendment passed. The vote on the ramp was taken by secret ballot and passed by a strong margin. The result of the conflict process was that everyone felt there was opportunity to influence the decision. No one was accused or blamed for positions held. Democratic ideals were upheld, and those who lost on the issue were satisfied with the fairness of the process.

These examples are not universal in application, nor are they regular occurrences in the life of a church. I see them rather as rare fulfillments of a valued belief, similar to the remarkable beauty of a cactus flowering under the most improbable conditions. The infrequency of the bloom in no way detracts from its natural appeal, but rather adds to its significance.

Rules for Fighting Clean in the Church

One of the causes of destructive conflict in the church is a lack of awareness of how to manage the differences. Anyone who plunges directly into a conflict without having prior agreement about its rules is asking for trouble. The result can be as vicious, dirty, and deadly as a street fight.

In the interest of respectful, clean, and healthful conflict in the church, consider these six rules which governed our budget meeting:

1. *Listen to each other, and "say it back."* A lot of time and energy are wasted in arguments when people misun-

derstand each other. Before parties can rebut an opponent's statements, they must first repeat the statement in their own words (see Chapter 6).

2. *Stick to the issues and stay away from personalities.* This is an ancient principle of parliamentary law found as early as 1604 in the proceedings of the House of Commons. The present wording of the Rule of Decorum in *Robert's Rules of Order* is:

> When a question is pending, a member can condemn the nature or likely consequences of the proposed measure in strong terms, but he must avoid personalities, and under no circumstances can he attack or question the motives of another member. The measure, not the man, is the subject of debate.[19]

3. *Stick to the present; do not bring up past conflicts.* This rule calls on church members to be as forgiving to each other as the Lord has been to them. Past hurts and resentments only cloud the issue.

4. *The best offense is a good defense.* State clearly your own position rather than attack an opposing position. "Float like a butterfly, sting like a bee" is not a healthy strategy for church conflict.

5. *If your position prevails, thank God. If your position is defeated, accept the majority decision and be patient.* Remember the advice of Gamaliel to the Jewish council: If you are correct, the truth will eventually come out. If you are wrong, you would be fighting against God (Acts 5:38-39).

6. *Remember that it is Christ's church, not yours or mine, and we are seeking God's will first.* Albert Curry Winn stated this most clearly:

In a truly missionary church, the function of church courts, conferences, conventions, or other deliberative bodies is not to get the will of my party voted, nor yet a compromise between my party and your party, but to determine if we can, the will of Christ.

That may well be difficult to determine, but we shall never determine it if we are seeking something else or something less.[20]

Openness to Conflict

An administrator who wants to move a church toward greater organizational health will be alert to the positive values of conflict along the way. This is a change from the older authoritarian approach to church life, in which the decisions of the elders and the pastor were simply announced and accepted. In most modern congregations a pluralistic mix of viewpoints exists which makes a traditional approach to decision making impossible. The servant-administrator encourages full discussion of important matters by anyone who wishes to express an opinion. As a voluntary organization, the church requires openness to conflict.

There was once a church which was having a terrible time resolving conflict among its members. When someone asked what the divisions were about, the reply came that there were strong doctrinal differences. One group believed that Pharaoh's daughter found the baby Moses in the bulrushes. The other group believed that was just what she had told her daddy.

More trivial issues than this young woman's credibility have divided churches. The point is that they need not divide. Full, reasonable discussion of an issue will bring it into the light by which mature Christians can make up their own minds. Often new, creative insights are founded on intense dialogue over divergent viewpoints in the church. As Lyle Schaller has suggested, "Conflict can help improve communication, prevent polarization, and shift the balance of power in an organization."[21]

By contrast, when conflict is absent, poor decisions are often hurriedly made. An important or costly project which is approved without any questioning or resistance could contain dangerous errors or oversights. Reports from the proceedings of the Kennedy administration before the unsuccessful Cuban Bay of Pigs invasion suggest that key advisers withheld dissenting views and significant questions for the sake of "unity."

A good biblical illustration of official openness to conflict is found in the story of King David's evacuation from Jerusalem during the rebellion of Absalom. As David was traveling away from the capital, he passed by the house of one of his old-time detractors named Shimei. This man not only despised the king, but he also had a very foul mouth, and he really loosed upon David a long tirade, liberally spiced with obscenity, about the king's low character. David's secret service agents quickly volunteered to go over and remove Shimei's head from his neck. At that point the great king was down, but he had not lost his wisdom. "Don't worry about it," he told his men. "This might be the Lord God speaking through Shimei. Everything else has gone wrong today; why should I expect any better? I will let him say what he wants, and wait for the Lord to change my fortunes" (2 Samuel 16:5-12, paraphrased).

One trait that served King David well was his openness to the will of God in times of crisis. He did not need to stifle human dissent. He knew patience would pay off eventually. The same trait is proposed for church members in this chapter—patience and openness to the leading of the will of God through human conflict.

Conclusion: Techniques of Administration—Removing Hindrances to the Leading of the Holy Spirit

"They traveled through the region of Phrygia and Galatia because the Holy Spirit did not let them preach the message in the province of Asia. That night Paul had a vision. . . ."

—Acts 16:6,9(TEV)

This book of "how to's" has been prompted by a real and present crisis. The mainline or established churches of our society are in need of revitalization. The essential resource for their renewal comes from God through the Holy Spirit, and that resource is readily available through faith. Many of us have seen how the Spirit can be rendered ineffective through a combination of human faults such as greed, pride, deceit, hatred, and lack of organizational skill. Because the church is a human organization, its servants need to know how to keep it in touch with its source of strength. The skills of followership and leadership, the most effective ways of working with committees and boards, the techniques of communication and conflict resolution—all have been beneficial to church life.

This book has not been one more text on management for church people. "Management" implies a way of controlling the results of organizational action. Church administrators do not have the luxury of being in control. Jesus told the story about someone who went away and left three servants with a portion of wealth to administer. Upon returning the owner called for an accounting of their administration. The accomplishments of the servants who made high rates of return on the money were noted and rewarded, but the fearful servant who locked up his share was treated with contempt and cast into the "outer darkness" (Matthew 25:14-30). Howard Thurman has commented that the servant was punished not for lack of results, but rather for lack of effort.

> We are never under obligation to achieve results. Of course, results are important and it may be that this is the reason effort is put forth. But results are not mandatory. Much of the energy and effort and many anxious hours are spent over the probable failure or success of our ventures. No one likes to fail. But it is important to remember that under certain circumstances, failure is its own success.
> To keep one's eye on results is to detract markedly from the business at hand. This is to be diverted from the task itself. It is to be only partially available to demands at hand. Very often it causes one to betray one's own inner sense of values because to hold fast to the integrity of the act may create the kind of displeasure which in the end will affect the results. However, if the results are left free to form themselves in terms of the quality and character of the act, then all of one's resources can be put at the disposal of the act itself.[22]

The techniques offered in this book are only what that term implies—skills or methods by which something is accomplished. Because the church is a human organization, many of the methods of other human organizations apply to its work. I suggest that church servants learn these skills well enough to act them out without calling attention to them. When the methods of management become the primary focus of a church servant, however, those methods can become as much a hindrance to accomplishing work in the church as the lack of skills. We know that teaching in the church requires the techniques discovered in secular education, but those techniques alone do not insure that the word of God is proclaimed in a classroom. The teacher's skills are integrated into the spiritual relationship with the students, and at best are only partially visible. So it should be for the skilled administrator.

The reader need not be confused over this discounting of results in the same book that has encouraged goal setting. Goals serve to raise the vision of a group and unite them as they are led by the Spirit. In Luke's version of the parable about the servants, the owner said to the servants as the gold was being distributed, "See what you can earn with this while I am gone" (Luke 19:13,TEV) Thus he set a goal as a direction and focus of effort. The accomplishments of the servants were recognized and duly appreciated by the owner. That was an evaluation of service. But the reward for the faithful servants was twofold; in addition to the opportunity of further responsibility (a new goal), they were invited to participate in the owner's joy. Church servants are called to faithful obedience rather than dependence on results. The distinction is real and significant.

The role of manager in the church is not filled by human servants, no matter what position they hold. Only the Holy Spirit can be called "manager."

> The Holy Spirit is not a useful tool or adjunct in a mission planned and designed by the church. He is the Lord of the mission. He is the Paraclete, Christ's presence in the church while Christ is absent. As, during the days of his flesh, Christ was not a useful tool in the disciples' mission but their Teacher and Director, so now the Holy Spirit is in charge. Since Christ is not here to send them out, the Holy Spirit becomes the Sender. With this the record in Acts agrees. There the Holy Spirit instigates and blocks and rechannels the mission of the church.[23]

Here is the meaning of the biblical basis for this conclusion. The results are controlled by the Holy Spirit. The task of the church's servants is to listen and follow.

Just how the Holy Spirit works in and through the human organization we know as the church could be the subject of a larger exploration. Such exploration is certainly needed since, as Richard Hutcheson observed, "the church does not have much in the way of a 'theology of organization.'"[24]

To summarize the thoughts of this book concerning the Church, let us project one "preview" film slide from a larger program of images in such an ecclesiology. Shown in this picture is a group of church members at a meeting. This is the church. It certainly is not the ideal church, for this slide shows real people with their limitations and faults. Yet here is the body of Christ. Here is an incarnation of God's presence, the way God has chosen to get work done in the world.

As you look around the room, you see that many members are participating in a discussion. Apparently a decision is to be made in this group about the mission of this local church. With so much involvement, the group must be organized in a fairly democratic way. Some of them have their Bibles open and are sharing their interpretations of a particular passage. Others are making comments and critiques on the viewpoints expressed by their colleagues. Since the time of the Reformation, Christians have been free in their own way to study and interpret the Bible, free to apply its teachings to life and to the church's mission according to conscience. Nobody has absolute authority to do this for them.[25]

By the looks on many of the faces, people are not only talking but they are also listening. We might call this "dialogue" (using Buber's term) or "creative interchange" (according to the term coined by Henry Nelson Wieman). As one person expresses an individual perspective on the issue, others engage in a kind of appreciative understanding in which they not only hear the words of expressers but fully grasp their meaning. This kind of "depth perception" allows for a transformation of the minds and hearts of both expresser and perceiver. What emerges from such an interchange is often a new idea or fresh insight which was not present in the mind of any of the participants earlier. In addition, a new sense of community is born in such interchange that is at the same time broader and more profound than can be explained by human togetherness. What has functioned in this interaction is the power of the Holy Spirit to liberate, perfect, and comfort Christians, to bestow gifts for the building up of the church, to bring a new sense of unity and peace, and to inspire with new vision the direction the work of the church will take.[26]

Try to determine, by observing the participants in this picture, which one is the leader in the group. Picking the leader is not easy, because that person does not operate as an authority but as a servant of the group. As servant, the leader has anticipated the issues and problems the group is facing and suggests structures and techniques that assist it in carrying out its task. Notice that an agenda for the meeting is printed on newsprint on the wall. On another sheet is the goal the group has worked out for discussion in this meeting. The leader is careful to watch and listen for those who dominate the conversation, and for those who are not participating at all. This leader knows that a silent member could be simply a good listener——or could be holding on to an idea or insight which is very important to the group. Several times the leader has encouraged members to share insights, especially if the insight seems to be at odds with the thinking of the rest of the group. We can almost hear the leader saying, "How do we know? You may be the only person in the room to whom the Holy Spirit has been able to get through with that insight!" By being a good "depth perceiver" the leader is modeling that listening process for others. In fact, such listening tends to bring out the leadership abilities of others in the group who share in the structuring and guiding of the conversation. That is one of the reasons it was so hard at first to pick out the acknowledged head of the group.

The meeting is nearly over at the time this slide picture is taken. The group will conclude its discussion and finalize its decision. We cannot tell whether there will be a vote and the majority will rule, or whether the group will arrive at a consensus or sense of the meeting. The method of decision making does not seem to matter. What is obvious is the sense of unity in the midst of diversity in this meeting. Folks are approaching their task with a sense of "we and ours" instead of "me and mine." That is one way to tell whether the Holy Spirit has been able to operate freely in the group, for the Bible says the gifts of the Spirit are given for "building up the body of Christ" (Ephesians 4:12).

Already we can observe that the decision the group is about to make is not perfect. We know that councils can err. Nevertheless, we can be comfortable with this imperfection when we recall two principles. First, the decision of the group is probably closer to the truth than would have been the decision of the leader alone, for we mistrust power placed in the hands of individuals without checks and balances. And, second, we recall that the church is judged by God on its genuine effort and not by its results.

Notes

[1]Presbyterian Church (U.S.A.), *Form of Government* (New York and Atlanta: Offices of the General Assembly, 1981), G-40201.

[2]Albert Curry Winn, *A Sense of Mission: Guidance from the Gospel of John* (Philadelphia: The Westminster Press, 1981), p. 55.

[3]Robert K. Greenleaf, *Servant Leadership: A Journey into the Nature of Legitimate Power and Greatness* (New York: Paulist Press, 1977), p. 218.

[4]The Presbyterian Church in the United States, *Our Confessional Heritage: Confessions of the Reformed Tradition with a Contemporary Declaration of Faith* (Atlanta: Materials Distribution Service, 1977), p. 166.

[5]Dietrich Bonhoeffer, *Life Together* (New York: Harper & Row, Publishers Inc., 1976), p. 29.

[6]John Savage, *The Apathetic and Bored Church Member* (Philadelphia: LEAD Consultants, 1976), pp. 64-67.

[7]David R. Sawyer, "The Construction and Evaluation of a Communicational Climate Questionnaire for Church Use" (Unpublished doctoral dissertation, Ohio University, 1979).

[8]Paul Hersey and Kenneth H. Blanchard, *Management of Organizational Behavior* (Englewood Cliffs, NJ: Prentice-Hall, 1982), p. 89.

[9]*Ibid.*, p. 248.

[10]*Ibid.*

[11]Adapted from J. William Pfeiffer and John E. Jones, eds., *A Handbook of Structured Experiences for Human Relations Training, Vol. IV* (La Jolla, Calif.: University Associates), p. 60.

[12]Reprinted from Malcolm and Hulda Knowles, *Introduction to Group Dynamics* (New York: Association Press, 1972), p. 53, copyright © 1972. Permission granted by New Century Publishers, Inc., Piscataway, NJ.

[13]David and Vera Mace, *What's Happening to Clergy Marriages?* (Nashville: Abingdon Press, 1980), p. 33.

[14]Wayne Oates, *Confessions of a Workaholic* (New York: World Publishing Co., 1971).

[15]*Ibid.,* p. 108.

[16]The United Presbyterian Church in the U.S.A., The Vocation Agency, *Pastoral Activities Index* (New York: The Vocation Agency, 1976).

[17]Robert R. Blake, Herbert Shepard, and Jane S. Mouton, *Managing Intergroup Conflict in Industry* (Houston: Gulf Publishing Co., 1964), pp. 12–13.

[18]Speed Leas and Paul Kittlaus, *Church Fights: Managing Conflict in the Local Church* (Philadelphia: The Westminster Press, 1973), p. 48.

[19]Henry M. Robert and Sarah Corbin Robert, *Robert's Rules of Order Newly Revised* (Glenview, Ill.: Scott Foresman & Co., 1981). pp. 331–332.

[20]Winn, *op. cit.,* p. 45.

[21]Lyle E. Schaller, *The Change Agent: The Strategy of Innovative Leadership* (Nashville: Abingdon Press, 1972), p. 167.

[22]Howard Thurman, *The Inward Journey* (New York: Harper and Row, Publishers Inc., 1961), p. 64.

[23]Winn, *op. cit.,* p. 97.

[24]Richard Hutcheson, Jr., *Wheel Within the Wheel: Confronting the Management Crisis in the Pluralistic Church* (Atlanta: John Knox Press, 1979), p. 244.

[25]Wolfart Pannenberg, *Theology and the Kingdom of God* (Philadelphia: The Westminster Press, 1969), p. 99.

[26]Winn, *op. cit.,* p. 98.

Bibliography

Blake, Robert R., Herbert Shepard, and Jane S. Mouton, *Managing Intergroup Conflict in Industry.* Houston: Gulf Publishing, 1964.

Bonhoeffer, Dietrich. *Life Together.* New York: Harper and Row, 1954.

Greenleaf, Robert K. *Servant Leadership: (A Journey Into the Nature of Legitimate Power and Greatness.)* New York: Paulist Press, 1977.

Halpin, A.W. *Theory and Research in Administration.* New York: The MacMillan Co., 1966.

Hersey, Paul, and Kenneth H. Blanchard. *Management of Organizational Behavior.* Englewood Cliffs, New Jersey: Prentice-Hall, 1969.

Hutcheson, Richard G., Jr., *Wheel Within the Wheel: Confronting the Management Crisis in the Pluralistic Church.* Atlanta: John Knox, 1979.

Knowles, Malcolm and Hulda. *Introduction to Group Dynamics.* New York: Association Press, 1972.

Leas, Speed, and Paul Kittlaus. *Church Fights: Managing Conflict in the Local Church.* Philadelphia: Westmin-